India's Knowledge Supremacy

India's Knowledge Supremacy

The New Dawn

Ashwin Fernandes

B L O O M S B U R Y
NEW DELHI • LONDON • OXFORD • NEW YORK • SYDNEY

BLOOMSBURY INDIA
Bloomsbury Publishing India Pvt. Ltd
Second Floor, LSC Building No. 4, DDA Complex,
Pocket C – 6 & 7, Vasant Kunj,
New Delhi 110070

BLOOMSBURY, BLOOMSBURY PRIME and the Diana logo are trademarks of Bloomsbury Publishing Plc

First published in India 2023
This edition published 2023

ISBN: 978-93-56402-69-0
2 4 6 8 10 9 7 5 3 1

Printed and bound in India by Replika Press Pvt. Ltd

To find out more about our authors and books, visit www.bloomsbury.com and sign up for our newsletters

For my mother, Evita

Through scorching summers and torrid rains,
Through life's smallest and greatest pains,
You taught me what I needed to know
You showed me where I had to go.

You instilled values in me of every kind
To think from the heart, not just the mind
You watched my ambition take flight
And pushed me with all your might.

Mama, everything I am is because of you
You make everything better, you really do.

Contents

Foreword

India, with a rich legacy going back thousands of years, has always laid emphasis on education and scholarship. Nalanda, established in the fourth century BCE, was an ancient centre of higher learning from 427 BCE to 1197 CE. By the seventh century CE, the university boasted of 3,000 teachers and 10,000 students from countries like China, Indonesia, Korea, Japan, Persia and Turkey, who had come to learn Buddhist studies, fine arts, medicine, astronomy, politics, and the art of war. Hiuen Tsang, the famous monk, scholar and traveller from China, visited Nalanda at that time to study and teach for five years. Tragically, a great fire wiped out the library which housed over 9 million manuscripts at the beginning of the 12th century. Over time, the glorious past of the country faded away due to several invasions which changed the very course of education. In the 16th century, the East India Company came to India primarily for business, but it ended up establishing a British empire in India. As the supremacy of the British in India increased, education in general was neglected. Macaulay's Minute of 1835 clearly stated the intentions of the British, wherein he mentioned that the purpose of education was to 'form a class who may be interpreters between us and the millions whom we govern; a class of persons, Indian in blood and colour, but English in taste, in opinions, in morals, and in intellect.'

In 1947, post-independence, India inherited an educational system which was rife with great educational disparities between men and women, upper and lower classes, and urban and rural populations. Many wide-ranging deliberations in conferences, committees and commissions were held to discuss the issues relating to providing access to quality education to all. The foremost was the Radhakrishnan Commission (1948–49) also known as University Education Commission which recommended that university education should aim at producing intellectuals who shall be able to direct, guide, preserve and revive the Indian culture and civilisation. Subsequent to this, the Kothari Commission (1964–66) also known as

National Education Commission, was constituted to formulate a coherent education policy for India. The commission recommended that education was intended to increase productivity, develop social and national unity, consolidate democracy, modernise the country and develop social, moral and spiritual values. As a result of the recommendations of the Kothari Commission, India formulated the first National Policy on Education in 1968 which called for a radical restructuring and proposed equal educational opportunities in order to achieve national integration. The policy advocated for free and compulsory education for all children up to the age of 14, the development of languages, the equality of educational opportunities and the development and prioritisation of scientific education and research. In 1986, the second National Policy on Education was issued which laid special emphasis on the removal of disparities and equalise educational opportunity. To achieve social integration, the policy called for expanding scholarships, adult education, recruiting more teachers from disadvantaged sections and developing new institutions.

The quality of higher education has been a perennial issue affecting our ability to build world-class higher education institutions. Apart from ensuring access and equity, internationalisation, global rankings, accreditation, assessment, and the benchmarking of institutions are the compelling factors impacting the quality of education. The struggle to offer world-class education has created immense pressure on higher education policy, regulation, and the governance of universities. A need for transformation in the education system was also triggered by the developments taking place around the world and the resultant changes ushered into our societies. Education in general and higher education, in particular, assumed a pivotal role in the process of this transformation. The developments in the education space gave rise to a competitive environment among the various countries of the world propelling them to rethink their priorities.

To address all these issues and to adapt to changes being faced by India in the global higher education space, a need was being felt for a new policy which takes into account the changing paradigms of higher education while being firmly rooted in its traditional knowledge systems. The National Education Policy 2020 is one such effort of the Government of India towards providing a precise roadmap to come out of the foggy situation prevalent in the higher education system of the country. The policy not only provides tangible and effective solutions for most of the problems ailing higher education in the country but also lays a clear path for future needs. It emphasises on education as being fundamental to human development and the high-quality learning opportunities that the nation must provide to its young minds to prepare them for the future. The policy endeavours to address the changing dynamics of the population's requirement with regards to providing quality education with a special focus on innovation and research to fulfil the objective of making India a knowledge superpower by equipping its students with the necessary skills, attitude and knowledge.

The book in hand, *India's Knowledge Supremacy: The New Dawn*, very clearly describes India's journey from ancient times to the present day and discusses using education as a soft power for making India a knowledge powerhouse of the world. It talks about ancient Indian wisdom when knowledge was blended with spirituality, the new paradigms emerging in the Indian higher education landscape and also the recent scenario when the production, dissemination, acquisition and assessment of knowledge are measured with rankings and accreditation.

I am confident that the suggestions provided in this book would be very helpful in re-envisioning our universities in sync with the educational needs of the 21st century and beyond, and that the readers will enjoy reading this book.

– Dr (Mrs) Pankaj Mittal
Secretary General
Association of Indian Universities

Preface

It was 24 September 2014; I was based in Singapore. I clearly remember the words of Prime Minister Narendra Modi on national television: '*Aaj MOM ka Mangal ke saath milan ho gaya. Aaj Mangal ko MOM mil gayi*.' Loosely translated to, 'Today MOM has met Mars. Today Mars has got a MOM.' What may seem like a simple play on words was indeed a historic moment for India. We had successfully reached Planet Mars in a maiden attempt through the Mars Orbiter Mission (MOM). What was more astounding is that the total cost of the mission was just under 4.5 billion rupees ($74m; £45m), which makes it one of the most cost-efficient interplanetary space missions ever.

In that moment, I realised that it was time to recognise India's rich history and to work towards bringing back the much-deserved glory to my motherland. A few weeks later, the *New York Times* published a cartoon depicting an Indian farmer with a cow knocking at the door of a room marked Elite Space Club where two men sat reading a newspaper on India's feat. It is ironic that 36 per cent of NASA's scientists are of Indian origin. At that moment, I also realised that it was time to return to my homeland to do bigger things in the area that I can influence: education.

A year later, in July 2015, my advocacy work brought me to meet the President of India at the time, Late Pranab Mukherjee. He was elated at having numerous Indian universities in the QS rankings. He was, of course, disappointed that none of the Indian universities was in the top 100. He mentioned that even though India has a good number of institutions, thousands of Indian students go abroad for higher education. 'We must reverse this trend,' he had said.

This book acknowledges the fact that India has had a glorious past, and despite the challenges faced by our economy for decades, we are seeing a reverse trend towards knowledge prosperity. I have made it my life's mission to take Indian higher education to the next level, and to bring several Indian institutions into the top 100 of global rankings. I will make the dream of our former President, and the ambitions of our current Prime Minister come true.

Indian civilisation is based on the value of seeking the truth, be it through spirituality or on a piece of paper. In the history of the world, India's contribution to the fields of mathematics, astronomy, language, and literature has been immense. This richness has been evident in numerous universities like Takshashila, Nalanda, Vallabhi and others. These institutions have been an immense source of knowledge where students from all over the world came to pursue education. The culture of oral teachings was well-established and there were no degrees to be sought or fixed time periods assigned to the students. There was no discrimination whatsoever among students. Brahmins who, according to mythology, were born out of Brahma's head, were the prime educators in those times. The Himalayan range stood as a great wall of protection and a barrier against evil, but danger came in with due time. Islamic invasions and plundering resulted in many universities across the Indian subcontinent being destroyed; manuscripts and scriptures were burnt.

Subsequently colonisation happened. Even before the British East India Company docked its ships on the shores of Calcutta, India had been discovered by Vasco da Gama. The Portuguese had come to India before the English. By the time they left, the Indian subcontinent had been fragmented.

The partition caused unprecedented massacres and violence. Millions of refugees crossed the borders amid chaos. The newly-born governments failed to take strategic steps in preventing the mayhem that ensued. As a result, education for many children got side-lined. Even after the formation of borders, India faced both international and domestic threats. Many different ideologies emerged, and some challenged the peace of India and its people. While tackling such serious issues, India set up universities and other educational institutions.

National educational policies passed by subsequent governments acted as stepping stones to a better education system. The diversity of India was captured somewhat by the education system, but flexibility in terms of inclusivity was still missing. Different governments have been working on this.

The National Education Policy of 2020 introduced a curriculum structure where students can gain knowledge as per their interests. Many programmes were introduced to provide skills to learners through high-quality education.

Under the leadership of Prime Minister Narendra Modi, traditions are meeting modernity in the educational sector. Finally, university students do not have to fit into a rigid structure. Instead, they can customise their education as per their preference. This initiative by the Ministry of Education has put smiles on the faces of millions of students and has thus weaved a better future for the country.

– Ashwin Fernandes

ONE

Learning Centres of Ancient India

Imparting Holistic Knowledge

India is the cradle of the human race, the birthplace of human speech, the mother of history, the grandmother of legend and the great-grandmother of tradition.

– Mark Twain

The Years Before Universities Were Built in India

Ancient India was a melting pot of languages, cultures, rituals and religions. Experiencing this rich and vibrant history of over 9,000 years requires a lot of appreciation. One can't stress enough the fact that India stood tall as a powerhouse of knowledge in the past.

The Indian educational system, like the country's culture and traditions, has a rich history. Knowledge was passed down from generation to generation, largely inspired by Hinduism. Brushing off the dust from ancient palm-leaf scripts, birch-bark texts and inscriptions, we have uncovered the ways knowledge and lessons were imparted in ancient India.

There was no formal education system in the past. A father passed on knowledge to his child, mostly connected to his profession. Much later, Vedic and Buddhist educational systems evolved. Teaching and learning were based on the Vedic and Upanishad ideals, which included duties to one's self, family and society. Indigenous education was disseminated at home, in temples, pathshalas and gurukuls.

Education in historic India was deeply rooted in rituals and customs, where the four Vedas (a collection of poems or hymns composed in archaic Sanskrit, which is also the parent language of many other languages) were taught to students. There are four Vedas: *Rigveda* (knowledge text of verses), *Yajurveda* (knowledge text of mantras), *Samaveda* (knowledge text of chants), and *Atharvaveda* (knowledge text of everyday life procedures). The Vedas are the religious texts which inform the religion of Hinduism (also known as Sanatana Dharma meaning 'Eternal Order' or 'Eternal Path'). The term 'Veda' means 'knowledge' and these texts are known to contain the fundamental knowledge relating to the underlying cause, function, and personal response to existence.

The Vedas have a rich history and are amongst the oldest religious works in the world. They are more commonly referred to as scriptures, which means they are the Holy Writ concerning the nature of the Divine. Unlike the scriptures of other religions, the Vedas were not revealed to a certain person at any specific time in history. Rather, they are believed to have been composed by sages in deep meditative states sometime prior to 1500 BCE. These are not only religious books of Hinduism, but also cover subjects like science, philosophy, meditation, and spirituality.

Praying to Goddess *Saraswati* (the goddess of knowledge) and God *Vinayaka* (the god of wealth and business) was supposed to aid those who were pursuing education. A *Guru* (Brahman saint) would take boys under his umbrella of knowledge, whereas girls were given education domestically, within a household. There were no home tutors to come and teach the girls about everything the boy studied, and this meant that they generally ran the household and did chores. The ancient times had their own set of orthodoxy and prejudices, and girls started to step out of the threshold of homes only when universities like Takshashila, Nalanda and Vallabhi were built. The Indian subcontinent saw the first co-education system when Takshashila was founded.

Before a boy's adulthood, the *Upanayana* (sacred thread ceremony) was conducted where the Guru would take the boy away from the household and impart to him knowledge of the world. The period after the *Upanayana* was called *Brahmacharya* (to live with oneself), and when a boy entered this period, he went through a period of rigorous exertions. The future of ancient India was built on reading sacred texts and following the words of Gurus.

Spirituality has been an integral part of the Indian culture for many centuries. In many parts of the world, India is still known as the birthplace of spiritualism. There were roughly 64 art forms in ancient India's schooling system, including dance, music, jewellery-making, sculpting, agriculture and medicinal sciences. In these various schools, men worked as trainees, under a master's supervision, in order to obtain vocational training in a particular art form. Science in ancient times was very different from modern science. With innovations such as keeping track of time through the sun clock or adding zero and pi to the field of mathematics, India was always at the forefront. In the field of medical science, too, India did not lag, and *Ayurveda* (medicine from natural substances) holistically healed, and continues to do so for people of all body and mind ailments.

The Indian subcontinent also gave birth to thinkers and seekers such as:

1. ***Aryabhatta:*** A mathematician and astronomer who was born in 476 BCE. He is known for his contributions to trigonometry, astronomy, and mathematics. In the field of mathematics, Aryabhatta's main contribution was the introduction of a place-value notation system for writing numbers. In his work, Aryabhatta described the decimal system, positional numeral system, irrational numbers, zero as a number and infinite series.
2. ***Banabhatta:*** A seventh century Indian poet who was born in Pritikuta, a village situated on the banks of Hiranyavahu. His work, Kadambari, is regarded as one of India's first books. It tells the story of a princess named Kadambari who falls in love with a Naga prince. Banabhatta was a Sanskrit poet and writer who wrote about emotions, nature and good triumphing over evil. He passed away before completing his final novel, Harsha Charita, an account of King Harsha in whose reign Banabhatta lived. In his remembrance, his son finished the task. Despite the fact that his major books Chandikasataka and Parvatiparinaya did not earn much critical recognition, they are alleged to have received several awards and distinctions.
3. ***Kalidasa:*** Kalidasa is considered to be ancient India's greatest poet and playwright. He wrote about love, war, politics, religion and other themes that were popular at that time. His works have been translated into many languages including English, French, German and Russian. While seven major works are attributed to him, there are countless numbers of writings which are said to be written by Kalidasa. Some of his famous works are Malavikaagnimitram (Malavika and Agnimitra), Vikramorvashiyam (The story of Urvashi and Pururavas) and Abhigyan Shakuntalam (Shakuntala). Although

most of Kalidasa's works are well known, Shakuntalam is regarded as the one that brought him widespread recognition. It was first translated into English from Sanskrit, then into German, and finally into several other Western languages.

4. ***Charaka:*** In the realms of Ayurveda, medicine and lifestyle, Charaka is a well-known figure. He is regarded as one of the pioneers of Ayurveda, and he contributed to the science and philosophy of the system. He is well known as the editor of the medicinal treatise Charaka Samhita, which is placed under Brhat-Trayi (early Sanskrit encyclopaedias of medicine and Ayurveda) and is considered one of the core books of ancient Indian medicine and Ayurveda.
5. ***Bhaskara II:*** Born in 1114 CE in Vijaypura, Bhaskara grew up to be a great mathematician and astronomer. In ancient India, he was the head of the astronomy observatory in Ujjain. During his lifetime, he was known as the leading mathematician in the country. Some of his works are *Lilavati* (The Beautiful), *Karanakutuhala* (Calculation of Astronomical Wonders), and *Bijaganita* (Seed Counting or Root Extraction).

Education During Adolescence

A child under the Vedic system began his schooling at the age of five. The Vidyarambha ritual was held to commemorate the beginning, which included worshipping Goddess Saraswati and learning the alphabet for the first time.

For a successful educational career, a boy had to pursue singlehood and determination. For this, another ritual known as Upanayana was performed, after which the young child left his parental home and moved in with his teacher. Brahmin, Kshatriya and Vaishya boys of various castes performed this ritual at various ages.

The teacher helped the student cultivate all elements of knowledge. Daily prayers, including a plethora of mantras, were a major part of the day. When a young boy began his journey into the sphere of knowledge, a *danda* (wooden stick) was handed to him, signifying self-reliance and the ability to guard himself against any untoward factors. Seeking and praying to the Divine was a way of sharpening the intellect. At the advent of puberty, when the hint of a beard began to appear, around 16 years of age, the boy was asked to go through a beard-shaving ceremony. Mantras were chanted and rituals were performed during the ceremony. This marked the beginning of a new phase for the young adult.

On the other hand, for young adults belonging to royalty, arriving at the age of 16 meant getting married. It also meant that by such time, the prince was supposed to have completed his studies. Naturally, the life of a prince was different from that of an ordinary boy. However, in both cases, the *Samavartana* (end of education) ceremony was performed, marking the end of education, akin to a graduation ceremony in today's age. This ceremony marked the end of the teacher's guidance, and it was time for the young adult to make decisions for himself and those around him.

Teacher and Student: A Holistic Relationship

The success of a student's education deeply depended on his relationship with his teacher. Not only did the student treat his teacher with utmost respect and gratitude, but the student's family also did the same. In ancient India, the value of a teacher was highlighted and recognised as education and knowledge were seen as significant aspects of life. A teacher was perceived as a channel or mode through whom one was awakened to both divinity and everyday life.

While parents were regarded as the source of the physical well-being of a child, a teacher was worshipped and was acknowledged as the spiritual guide, as it was he who would provide all the tools to live and learn in life through many different perspectives. Dharma was not a rigid structure for society; rather, it was a flexible concept that changed. The change, however, was slow. The spiritual father (teacher) would unveil the mysteries and introduce ways for the students to lead a balanced, calm and dharmic life. Not only Hinduism but also Buddhism upheld Dharma as an approach to life.

Spirituality and morality go hand-in-hand in the Vedas. As part of teaching, the priest or teacher would reverberate mantras to awaken the cosmos, along with different ceremonies which were conducted with bonfires. These chants were supposed to reach the ears of the Supreme. The heightening of energy through mantras, rituals and chants was performed towards sharpening the senses and seeking spiritual knowledge. This also helped the students to realise and understand how to conduct themselves, and other aspects of life that are related to spirituality.

Time is highlighted in the Vedas; it is the very source of existence. The word 'Brahman' was referred to as the supreme power. The Sun was regarded as God, and its impact on life was immense. Thus, students performed the *Surya Namaskar* (Sun Salutation) to pray to the Sun God for blessings. The phases of the Moon were also recorded to determine low and high tides, along with monitoring the planetary movements around the Sun; all these were factors in the course of human life as the planetary movements influenced people.

The Vedas were orally taught to students; this tradition continued even after writing became part of student life. Only a qualified teacher could teach the correct pronunciation and accent of the Vedas, and Vedic recitation was given maximum importance. Equally important was the role of the teacher or the Guru. The spiritual and philosophical aspects of a teacher were critical as it is through these traits that the students gained knowledge and wisdom. Learning through a Guru was given much more importance than learning through the written script. There was apprehension about studying books, as these were formed out of easily perishable and fragile substances like dried palm leaves and tree bark. The life experience of a Guru could not be compared with ordinary manuscripts.

An accomplished teacher was supposed to have recited the *Gayatri Mantra* (an invocation to the Supreme) more than 12,000 times. One-on-one teaching sessions were practised, and a student was given individual training along with group discussions and debates, the performance of which was rated as tests and examinations. A student was always encouraged to compete, with the aim of improving. If a student showed early signs of diligence and genius, he would also be given the task of taking lessons for younger students. The absence of training schools did not dull the preparation for higher education as the efficiency of the teacher mattered the most in bringing out the best in his students.

The way the children were transformed under the teachers' guidance was the primary factor which drove parents to choose a particular teacher over others. A good teacher received much appreciation. Most teachers were often married men. Through word of mouth, the abilities of a teacher would spread, and this aided parents to decide who their children's Guru would be. In turn, the Guru would judge a student's competence before taking him under his tutelage. Since the caste system was prevalent in ancient India, students were often even selected according to their family background and caste.

Income and Lifestyle of Teachers

In ancient India, teachers were given a *Guru Dakshina,* an offering, in return for teaching. The offering was made as per the prosperity of the student's household. If a student belonged to a rich family, then the Guru was offered more Dakshina than what a student from a poor family could offer.

The Guru Dakshina was a source of income for the teachers. They lived a simple life and, along with the Dakshina, donations from rulers or villagers for their contributions to educating the young ones of society were enough for them to get by. Some of the teachers were far removed from the temptations of life and would lead an alternate life to live as *sannyasins* (people who renounce the world). Living in the jungles and the experiences gathered therefore were an immense source of light for higher education for the students.

The discovery of a few inscriptions from the 11th and 12th century, in south India, gave a glimpse of the teachers' income. It was found that when educational institutions were established, Sanskrit colleges would give one-third *kalam* (a unit of measurement in ancient times) to one *kalam* of paddy at the end of each day to a teacher. Thus, in a month, a teacher, on average, would get around forty *kalams* of paddy. Annually, it would be something like four hundred and eighty *kalams* of paddy. Luxuries were not a part of the minds of teachers. The dignity, praise and respect they received as a teacher made their ordinary lives special.

The Emergence of Universities and Co-education

One of the earliest universities noted in ancient India was Vallabhi University. Established in 600 CE, the university was situated in present-day Bhavnagar, Gujarat. With years passing by, the Indian subcontinent saw the emergence of many universities that would support higher education for both boys and girls.

Higher education in ancient India, just like today, was connected with universities and other institutes of education. The universities attracted not only Indian students but also students from China, Sri Lanka, Nepal, Pakistan and Arabia. When a child reached the age of 16, he or she could take the university entrance examinations, which were quite a challenge. A system of co-education was introduced—this was done to encourage girls and uplift the social status of women in ancient India.

While there was no strict fee system, if a student failed to pay fees, then he or she could compensate for it by doing some work for the teacher.

When the rest of the world was yet to build organised educational institutions, the universities of ancient India already had scholarship programmes to assist meritorious students.

Education was accessible without any judgements regarding a student's family background, caste, gender or creed. Every student was equal in the universities where merit was the only ground on which they were judged. After completing primary education through the Gurukul system, students would undertake the admission test to various universities. Some of them even shifted from their hometown to complete their education, at a time when transport was not as advanced as nowadays. From 2000 BCE until the Islamic invasions, the map of India became a fertile land for budding universities. Apart from the four famous universities—Takshashila, Nalanda, Vallabhi and Vikramashila—there were many other regional universities too.

Prominent Ancient Universities of India

Name of Universities in Ancient India	*Location*	*Time When it was Founded*	*Time When it was Destroyed/Closed*
Telhara	Bihar	1st century BCE (built by descendants of Bimbisara, a Magadha ruler)	1193 CE (burnt by Bakhtiyar Khilji)
Takshashila	Taxila (near the banks of Indus River), now modern-day Pakistan	10th century BCE (founded by Chandragupta Maurya)	5th century CE (destroyed by Kidara Huns)
Nalanda	Bihar	5th century CE (built by King Kumargupta of Gupta Dynasty)	1193 CE (burnt by Bakhtiyar Khilji)
Valabhi	Gujarat	600 CE (built by Bhattarka, a Maitraka ruler)	1400 CE (attacked by the Mleccha Army)

Name of Universities in Ancient India	*Location*	*Time When it was Founded*	*Time When it was Destroyed/Closed*
Vikramashila	Bihar	783 to 820 CE (founded by emperor Dharmapala of the Pala Dynasty)	1203 CE (burnt by Bakhtiyar Khilji)
Sharada Peeth	Jammu and Kashmir	237 BCE (built by Raja Lalitaditya)	12th century CE (destroyed by Sikander Butshikhan)
Pushpagiri Vihara	Orissa	3rd century CE (built by Ashoka, a Mauryan emperor)	11th century CE (destroyed by Bakhtiyar Khilji)
Odantapuri	Bihar	8th century CE (built by Gopala I, ruler of the Pala Dynasty)	Late 12th century CE (destroyed by Bakhtiyar Khilji)
Mithila	Bihar	Flourished between 12th to 15th century CE (founded by Janaka)	15th century CE (destroyed by the Mughals)
Somapura Mahavihara	Bihar	7th century CE (founded by Dharmapala)	12th century CE (destroyed by foreign invaders, who set it on fire)
Morena Golden Triangle	Madhya Pradesh	8th century CE (built by the Gurjara-Pratihara Dynasty)	12th century CE
Kanthalloor Shala	Tamil Nadu	9th century CE (constructed under the Aayi Kingdom)	12th century CE (attacked by the Cholas)
Nadia	Bengal	—	—
Nagarjuna Vidyapeeth	Andhra Pradesh	7th century CE (built by Nagarjuna)	8th century CE (destroyed by Bakhtiyar Khilji)

Takshashila

About

Before a city becomes insignificant due to the erosion of time, it has led a bustling life. The same was the case with Taxila, a city near the Indus River, a seat of higher education. The great Chandragupta Maurya, founder of the Mauryan Empire in ancient India, and his court's wise council, Chanakya, were the founders of an institution for higher education called the Takshashila University. The ruins of it still remain, and it is of great interest to historians and archaeologists. Now in Pakistan, it was formerly a part of the Indian subcontinent prior to the partition, in 1947. Three major trade routes touched the city in the past: the *Uttarapath* or the North Route, the North-western route, and the route from Kashmir and Central Asia. The term Takshashila means 'severed head'. The Chinese traveller Faxian visited Taxila around 400 CE, and wrote that Taxila or 'the severed head' was the site of an incident in the Buddha's life where 'he gave his head to a man.'

The two great epic stories of India, Ramayana—the life story of Lord Ram—and the Mahabharata—the battle of Kurukshetra—have references to Taxila. Students from faraway and neighbouring lands flocked to study at Takshashila as it was renowned for being a powerhouse of intellect, attracting bright students from all around the world. The excellence of its teachers and the tranquil nature of the university attracted many students from lands like Magadha, Kosala and Kashi. Amidst the peace and quiet, students found the perfect place to study subjects like astrology, law, military science and medicine. Along with these subjects, skills like hunting and archery were also taught.

While the Vedas were dominant in the courses in the early years, the Buddhist scriptures were also made part of the courses later on. It is recorded that more than 10,500 students from around the world came to study at Takshashila in its lifetime. Pupils from Greece, China, Babylonia and Arabia mingled with the customs and cultures of the Indian subcontinent, as over 60 different courses were taught. The students had the freedom to select whichever subjects they wanted to learn. Mathematics, warfare, astronomy, politics, religion, philosophy and music were some of the subjects offered.

Administration

Experts in their own fields and famous teachers resided in and around the Taxila region. It became a hotspot of higher education due to the excellence of its teachers. The long and arduous journey to reach Takshahsila did not stop its students from going there in the pursuit of education. The rulers or local leaders did not influence the workings of the institution, and the university gave full autonomy to its teachers as they were regarded as the pillars of the institution. From its day-to-day work to course duration, everything was under the teachers' control, including the rules and regulations of the university and the decisions regarding the selection and rejection of students. Conflicts of interest were non-existent amongst its teachers as each specialised in their own field.

The students followed the directions of the teachers. The environment of Takshashila was not regimented. When the students became adequately informed, the teachers stopped teaching the course. The intellect of the students mattered in determining the course duration, as it was found that a specialised course would take around eight years to finish. No degrees were given on the completion of a course, and there were also no formal examinations at the end of the duration. Mastering units of a particular subject was very important. To proceed to the next chapters, a student had to master the previous one and each unit of a subject was meant to be thoroughly studied. If a teacher found that a student's capabilities did not match the qualities required to study the course, then he or she was asked to leave.

Nature of Education

Only higher education was taught at Takshashila University. Before getting admitted to the university, it was expected that the student would finish their secondary studies. Primary and secondary education was taught at homes and in hermitages. The age group of students was between 16 to 20 years. A wide variety of subjects—from scientific to literary—were available for students to choose from. Silpas (the science of arts and crafts) and Vedas were the main scientific and literary courses. The Brahmans were determined to preserve the Hindu culture and thus, learning the Vedas by heart was crucial for all students. It is found that out of the four Vedas, *Atharvaveda* was left out of the courses. This was most probably because knowledge in the Atharvaveda was part of many subjects. To ease the comprehension of Vedas, a number of books were written. Six sciences were included in the Vedas—aphoristic literature, the science of right pronunciation, astronomy, grammar, etymology and prosody.

The courses remained unchanged till the university existed. When religions, society, or politics required the addition of a topic, the curriculum was changed. There was a period of 1,500 years of work. After Taxila was vanquished by the Persians, the teachers were broadminded enough to welcome the Greek language as one of its subjects. Many invasions followed later on, and it is unknown to what extent the length of the curriculum of Takshashila was altered. However, all historians accept the great influence of Buddhism on the Takshashila courses.

The inclusion of Buddhism as a topic must have been done in order for the academics studying at the school to effectively dispute Buddhist teaching. The Scholars studied it to falsify the teachings of Buddhism. In arts, crafts and science, a student had to study theory as well as practice. In order to assist their pupils to obtain the essential abilities in their chosen area of study, teachers taught theory backed by a practical demonstration. However, the real practice of any art shows some fundamental concepts, which had to be deferred and left to the students' own talents and ingenuity to discover. It is critical in specialised fields like medicine to ensure that students have expertise in their subject, so that they will be able to prevent potentially dangerous events.

Teachers and Students

The teachers at Takshashila were not only knowledgeable in their fields but they also took the time to teach other teachers what they knew. They helped each other out with their knowledge and skills to make sure that everyone learned what they needed to know. It is considered to be one of the earliest universities in the world. Takshashila University was founded by Chanakya, who was also known as Kautilya. Chanakya had a vision for what he wanted Takshashila University to be like. He wanted it to have a large, central library with many books on different subjects such as mathematics, politics and economics.

He also wanted students to have separate living quarters that were located outside of town so they could focus on their studies and their goal of becoming educated, without distractions from other people or places. Three great teachers were part of the Takshashila University—Charak, a famous physician, Kautilya himself, who was also known as a famous

Sanskrit grammarian, and Panini, a famous scholar of Sanskrit and the founder of Sanskrit grammar.

Nalanda

About

The kingdom of Magadha was under the rule of Kumargupta, a ruler of the Gupta Dynasty when the Nalanda Mahavira University was built and founded. Other rulers and scholars like King Harshavardhana of Kannauj and the rulers of Pala patronised the university. Magadha falls under the modern-day Bihar, in India. Spread across thirty acres of land and mostly open in its architecture, Nalanda was a jewel in the capital of Magadha, called Rajgir. It is known from Buddhist scriptures that Buddha once visited the suburbs of Rajgir called Nalanda.

The name 'Nalanda' is an amalgamation of two words: Nalam and Da. The former means lotus and the latter means giving; the lotus is a symbol of knowledge. Therefore, Nalanda means giving knowledge. Stacking brick over brick in the fifth century, Nalanda came into being. From head to toe, the university was based on Buddhism but it attracted the attention of both Buddhist and non-Buddhist people. Students from China, Korea, Tibet, Sri Lanka, Mongolia, Japan, Turkey and other parts of Central Asia travelled a long distance to study at Nalanda University. Invasions and plunders destroyed the university three times. However, sadly, it was rebuilt only twice.

The university had a very well-stocked up library where manuscripts were stored with much care. From traditional sources of Tibet, it is known that the Nalanda library had four sections: *Dharmaganja* (Piety Mart), *Ratnodadhi* (Sea of Jewels), *Ratnasagara* (Ocean of Jewels) and *RatnaRanjak* (Jewel-adorned). Estimations by historians have found that the number of volumes in the library may have crossed hundreds of thousands. According to historical sources, the university survived eight hundred years, from the 5th to the 12th century CE. It is believed that there were 200 teachers and 10,000 pupils on the site. The historic architecture of Nalanda University demonstrated the blending of nature and man, where man-made structures were smoothly integrated into the natural environment, implying connections between the living and the location where knowledge was transmitted. Scholars of this university left behind documents and records of the architecture, ambience and educational environment of the university. With such jewels of wisdom on the site, Nalanda was definitely one of the best universities of ancient times, catering to Buddhist culture, learning and teaching burgeoned to manifest higher education in students.

The learning centre also had ten temples, lakes, meditation rooms, parks and classrooms. The monks in the university copied books meticulously so that all professors could have their own set of books. The university had eight colleges and each college was built by eight different scholars of ancient India. Scholars were called *Vidyanuragis* and out of the eight architects, *Balaputradeva,* the king of Sumatra, was chief. Apart from manuscripts, the monks at Nalanda also kept records through inscriptions. One such inscription called *Yashovarma* had beautiful remarks on the architecture and structure of the university. It is said that the university had an observatory that touched the sky.

Administration

A knowledgeable, wise and experienced monk (*bhikkhu*) was picked by the city's Buddhist congregations to lead the institution. Though two councils were constituted for this purpose, the bhikkhu led and directed the job of governing university matters, academic, administrative, and otherwise. One council oversaw duties like assigning students to the university, governing courses in various subjects, assigning work to teachers, holding regular examinations, and securing and maintaining manuscripts, as well as the scheme for copying manuscripts, which were in high demand at the time. Another council oversaw finances, building development and repairs, obtaining and delivering food, and allocating clothing to pupils and teachers based on their standing. Colleges were full of hardworking students, and the labour required to run the institution was shared. The councils' main responsibilities were leasing property to farmers, gathering maize from renters, and distributing it to other organisations. Despite the fact that it was a federation of many organisations, each one retained its autonomy and efficacy. Unlike Hindu institutions, which were secluded and reliant on a master's transmission of knowledge, these colleges had banded together into bigger groups known as *viharas* (monasteries). This law ensured that all colleges under their control functioned independently while retaining essential linkages. The federation developed norms that regulated both instructors and students, keeping in mind not just intellectual controversies but also healthy professorial relations. They wanted to keep the mood intellectual because each teacher was autonomous of the federation, and they were able to make their own disciplinary judgments. Nalanda University was a mixed bag of restrictions and jurisdiction.

Nature of Education

The university's curriculum was rather extensive, allowing students to study both Buddhist and non-Buddhist disciplines. It offered a variety of classes for people interested in learning more about *Mahayana* (a term for a broad group of Buddhist traditions, texts, philosophies, and practices) or *Vinaya Buddhism* (a set of disciplinary precepts for monks and nuns to refrain from worldly affairs such as cussing, drinking alcohol, sexual activity). It was necessary to learn Mahayana Buddhism, as well as to study all 18 schools of Buddhism and grapple with the ideas of *Sunyava* and *Vijnanavada* (both schools of literature). The Mahayanists believed that items appear to exist only for a short time before they are destroyed. The philosophy is known as 'Skyflower.' The Hinayanists, on the other hand, consider this view to be a heretic doctrine. There are also ethical and disciplinary teachings that are solely adhered to by Mahayana Buddhists. Nonetheless, given the importance of dialectics at the time, it must have played an important role in the institution. College of reasoning and astronomy were the other offerings. Tantra was a popular topic at this institution, and students learned from numerous academics who were producing works on it. Mantras, Mudras, Dharanis, Samadhi (different Vedic scriptures) and Yoga were not part of primordial Buddhism, and no form of worship was prescribed. Instead, the Buddha concentrated on achieving Nirvana, or insight into the true essence of existence, which guaranteed deliverance from suffering. Courses in the Vedas and its six auxiliaries were part of the curriculum. Additional classes in medicine, grammar, Sankhya, philology, law and philosophy were also held. There were a variety of other topics too, including those from the Buddhist and Brahmanical traditions, as well as more secular arts.

Teachers and Students

It is estimated that there were 10,000 monks at Nalanda University. They educated pupils who were divided into different ability levels and disciplines. On average, there were around a 100 lectures every day. This would imply seven or eight pupils per teacher, making it much simpler to help each student personally. Nalanda University's learned men were well-known across India. They enlightened numerous pandits on the path to Buddhism. Hieun Tsang, who studied Indian religions and, to a lesser extent, Buddhism, as well as other faiths such as Kapalikas, Jatakas, and Sankhyas, was one of them.

Vallabhi

About

The University of Vallabhi was established in the western part of India, in Gujarat. It resembled the Wala state in a number of ways. It was a significant Buddhist centre that had championed Hinayana Buddhism. Vallabhi was a competitor of Nalanda in the education sector for a while, and it enjoyed a period of prominence when it was the capital of the Maitraka rulers, who reigned from 480 to 775 CE.

Nature of Education

Hinayana teaching was taught along with other religious sciences. This university attracted Brahman students from the Gangetic plains. In addition to theological themes, students studied politics, business, agriculture and other topics. In rare situations, kings enlisted the aid of university students to help with governmental matters.

Teachers and Students

There were 6,000 monks learning at this institution, and they were given 100 monasteries to reside in. According to the *Kathasaritsagara*, an 11th century Indian epic poem about prince Kama's love, life and adventures, Vallabhi had become so well-known as an educational institution that a Brahman sent his child to Vallabhi instead of Nalanda or Banaras. Except for the names of two of the institution's scholars, Sthiramati and Gunamati, not much is known about the university.

Vikramashila

About

Before Nalanda University came into existence, the Vikramashila Vihara was a significant Buddhist monastery. It was located on the Ganga's banks, north of Magadha (Bihar). Pala monarch Dharmapala founded this educational college in the seventh century, around 50 kilometres east of Bhagalpur in Bihar. Education was a top priority for the Pala monarchs of ancient Bengal and Bihar. Vikramashila University attracted students from all across the country as well as a few foreign countries. At this old university, over 100 professors taught over 1,000 pupils. It was filled with temples, as were all old colleges. The numerous temples were overseen by 108 scholars of the university. For the temples and learning centre, additional *acharyas* (expert instructors) were chosen. The Mahastasthavir or Kulpati, who was normally elected, was the university's highest authority. There were six large colleges, each having a large structure and a large classroom. Vigyan Bhawan was the name given to the major structure and gates linked all of the structures. At the main gate, a *dwar pandit* (entrance priest) was assigned to keep watch. His job entailed examining people who applied for admission to the university.

Administration

There were several boards that are responsible for various parts of the university's day-to-day operations. The titular president was in charge of all of them. Teachers were given total academic freedom and were in control of their departments' work. Teachers used to admit only the best students as the university would first offer them a test to ensure that they were qualified. Each entrance was guarded by one of the six professors, who ensured that the quality of their education was on par with that of the other levels. Six famous logicians were commissioned to study various issues during Chankya's existence. The gates were Ratnakarasanti to the east, Vagisvarakirti to the west, Naropa to the north, Prajnakaramati to the south, Ratnavajra in front of the first gate, and Jnanasrimitra in front of the second.

Nature of Education

This university, like others, provided college-level training in specific disciplines. The bar for admission to this institution was quite high. They would only accept someone who wanted to become a Buddhist and then preach in other places. As the name implies, this Buddhist institution advocated the Mahayana sect, a broader style of Buddhism. This Buddhist monastery, being a Mahayana institution, must have also taught Hinayana Buddhism and taught writings that may be regarded as belonging to either or both streams of Buddhism. Other fields of Hindu knowledge were also taught in addition to these. However, they were not Buddhist in nature.

Teachers and Students

The university's professors were well-known both within and outside of India for their expertise. As a result, the institution developed a number of literary and cultural collaborations. Tibet's scholars have long been interested in Tantra, therefore they organised for it to be taught at the university. This continued for 400 years. Vikramashila was the birthplace of Tibetan culture. Its intellectuals made significant contributions to the progress of Tibetan civilisation as protectors of religion, society and education. Experts at the university authored books in Sanskrit on diverse subjects, and some even transcribed them into Tibetan. Some of these academics are believed to have published over 200 volumes, including both originals and translations. Dharmapala, the university's first patron, chose a total of 114 instructors, including 108 professors and other experts.

Descriptions of a Few Other Universities

Mithila University

Not much is known about this university which was in existence during the rule of King Janak. He was the father of Sita (wife of Lord Ram). The dearth of archaeological findings is the reason why historians and archaeologists are still struggling to discover more. King Janak used to hold religious meetings and conferences with rishis and other scholars. The university was a hotspot where subjects like science, fine arts and scriptures were taught. Vedas and *Nyaya Shastra* were two of the many scriptures heavily discussed at the university. A school was added to the site in the 12th century. It was founded by a great Indian philosopher and mathematician, Gangesa Upadhyaya, to teach logic. Gangesa Upadhyaya wrote one of his best works in the university called *Tattva Chintamani* (A Thought-jewel of Truth). The university later on appended two other subjects called *tarka shashtra* (logic) and *nyaya* (jurisprudence).

Telhara University

In the year 2009, a group of archaeologists started to excavate the Telhara region which is around 40 kilometres away from Nalanda University. After five years of extreme labour and patience, the ruins of Telhara University emerged. Many historians have given credit to the journals and writings of Hiuen Tsang which mentioned that Telhara University was a huge competitor of Nalanda University. Apart from providing higher education to the students, in-depth research also took place in the learning centre. Knowing more about the world and beyond was always cherished among scholars and students of the university. The foundation of the university drew a new story. From the bricks and clay sprinklers, archaeologists concluded that it was built before Nalanda University. Tantric Buddhism was cultured in the prayer hall of the three-storey building. It is believed that the university is 3,000 years old and was destroyed by Bakhtiyar Khilji. The ASI team during the excavation found a one-and-a-half foot layer of ashes. In 1193 CE, the invasion and plunders of Bakhtiyar Khilji and his army destroyed three universities, and Telhara was one of them.

Pushpagiri University

Pushpagiri University was built in the last years of BCE. In ancient India, the region was called Kalinga and presently it is located across the districts of Jajpur and Cuttack, Odisha. The university was older than Nalanda University and many claims that it was established by the great Emperor Ashoka. Udayagiri, Ratnagiri and Lalitgiri are the hills where the campus of the university spread. Students from across the world were welcomed into the learning centre. The king made offerings and donations to the university just to erect a stone mandapa at the learning site. The university could not sustain itself due to the lack of donations after Islamic invasions.

Odantapuri University

This university was established in Magadha around the seventh century by Gopala, a Pala king. Odantapuri University admitted international students along with Indian students but it was not as popular and famous as Nalanda University. Some Tibetan sources claim that the university could accommodate 12,000 students. Subjects ranged from Sanskrit to science, and Vedas were embedded in the university curriculum. Acharya Ganga, who was a scholar at Vikramashila, was formerly a student at Odantapuri University. The name Odantapuri comes from Uddandapura, a place in Bihar.

Sharada Peeth University

Sharada Peeth University was one of the most renowned institutions of learning in the world. It was not just a university but also a temple. The university was built in 237 BCE by Raja Lalitaditya Muktapida and the south door of the university was opened by the great sage Shankaracharya and was a centre for the study of Vedic texts and philosophy. The institution was named after the goddess of knowledge, Saraswati. Even though it was founded during the reign of Ashoka, the university was built during the Kushan reign. While the institution has always been famous, throughout the reigns of Maharaja Ranbir Singh and Pratap Singh, the yearly pilgrimage to the temple flourished. Currently the ruins of it fall in Pakistan-administered Kashmir. The site was abandoned after India and Pakistan went to war between 1947–48. At one point, there were 5,000 scholars residing at the university which also housed the world's biggest library. History, logic, structural science, geography and philosophy were taught there along with Buddhism. It is said that the university was once on par with Takshashila and Nalanda.

Changes in the Education System Post-Buddhist Era

It is interesting to note that the Buddhist period saw the emergence of many eminent scholars in different fields like mathematics, literature, astronomy, medicine and philosophy. This period also saw the development of many Sanskrit texts on these subjects. Many universities were established by Indian rulers who wanted to provide opportunities for higher education to all sections of society, irrespective of caste or creed. Buddhist education aspired to transform individuals by teaching them to be ethical, intellectual and spiritual beings. The Buddhist times also saw a great deal of experimentation in education with some thinkers arguing for formal schooling while others arguing against it. Buddhist monasteries and institutions played important roles in the development of Buddhist education, which focused on developing a person's intellect and values.

The Buddhist Era in India was marked by a shift from traditional Vedic education to the study of Buddhism. The Vedic education system focused on teaching students about rituals and sacrifices, while the Buddhist educational system focused on teaching students about meditation, philosophy and ethics. After foreign invasions, most of which were Islamic ones, the higher education system went through changes and turmoil. The invasions destroyed many institutions and shook the higher educational system.

In the post-Buddhist Era, the education system in India underwent many changes. It was changed to suit the needs of the people and it was also made accessible and compulsory for all levels of people. With the spread of Islam, a new set of education policies were introduced to India that made it more focused on religious studies than on general knowledge. As a result, Indian scholars shifted their focus from Sanskrit texts to Arabic texts which resulted in many Indian scholars being able to read and write the Arabic language. The curriculum followed a pattern that included learning Arabic, Persian and Urdu languages as well as learning Indian history from a Muslim perspective. Maktabs and madrassas were built as Islamic educational institutions. In these learning centres, grammar, mathematics, philosophy, science, law humanities and Islamic scriptures were taught. During the reign of Akbar, the third emperor of the Mughal dynasty, Indian scholars like Charaka, Patanjali and Bhaskara were respected. Thus, even though the Islamic influence stayed, the original language of India and its rituals were sustained. However, Aurangazeb, the sixth emperor of the Mughal dynasty, wanted the education system to be shifted to the subjects that were linked to administration. The vision of the different rulers altered the future of the entire education system of the Indian subcontinent.

TWO

The Lost Lustre

Indian Education During British Era

> **We must at present do our best to form a class who may be interpreters between us and the millions whom we govern; a class of persons, Indian in blood and colour, but English in taste, in opinions, in morals, and in intellect.**
>
> **– Lord Macaulay**

The Arrival of East India Company and its Language

Sailing in with their ships and arriving in India to trade, the East India Company (EIC) brought the English language along with them. The Indian subcontinent always welcomed foreigners and their languages, but the arrival of the English and their culture was to put a heavy mark on the people of India for centuries to come.

Spread across many different regions, kings in the Indian subcontinent battled with each other to capture more territory. Religion became a political matter. Rajput rulers sided with their kind; territories were annexed by the Islamic rulers. Much later, the fall of the Mughal dynasty divided a major part of India into further smaller fragments. The Mughals pushed their rule as much as they could. The East India Company came to India to trade in Indian spices, and soon enough they took interest in the political system of India. In the year 1612, the company defeated the Portuguese and ceased the concessions to trade from the Mughals. As trade started to flourish, the company needed more people to fit into its administrative system. Bringing Englishmen from their home country meant more expenses, especially when India offered cheap labour.

Colonisation and English Influence

The East India Company was an uninvited guest determined to stay for many decades to come. Over time, this started affecting the Indian society and its education system too. English influence started to emerge first in Bengal, where Calcutta, the capital, was the initial place the East India Company established its project in.

South India cultivated a huge number of Indian spices. Loading them onto their ships, the company started to export them to different parts of Europe and the rest of the world. India was the land of cheap labour, and the EIC wasted no time in appointing and recruiting Indian men into their clerical posts, along with hiring them for manual labour.

In ancient India, higher education in universities was provided orally by great scholars and professors. There were very few universities that had collections of books, manuscripts and scriptures. Tales and legends were passed on from one generation to the other, orally. It was only during the Buddhist and Islamic eras that writing was promoted. The colonisation of British India cemented the importance of writing in the Indian culture forever. Higher education became more concrete and systematic. The Gurukul system, where classes were held in private rooms of teachers, started to vanish. The 1800s saw the establishment of colleges where English was taught. Degrees in English gained more importance than most other subjects.

The English Education Act 1835

The English Education Act 1835 came into existence as a legislative act of the Council of India. Modernisation was channelled into the Indian education system through the legislation of the British Parliament, by Lord William Bentinck, who was the governor-general of the East India Company at that time. After the passing of the Education Act by the British Parliament, funds were allocated to be spent on higher education in India, with the idea to prioritise English as the main language. The East India Company allocated 100,000 rupees per year to introduce English literature into the education system. Westernisation and modernisation of the Indian education system were bound to have long-term effects.

In the year 1854, the president of the Board of Control of the East India Company, Sir Charles Wood, sent a despatch to Lord Dalhousie, the then governor-general of India, which was termed the Magna Carta of English education in India. He recommended many crucial points that would push Indian education to be more English language-oriented. Wood's despatch asked the government to take responsibility for Indian education.

Regularising the Education System up to University Level

From primary schools to the university level, British influence struck strongly on the Indian education system. As the Indian government was run by the British, the English language received a place of prominence in society. If a person knew English, they were eligible for a clerical or administrative post in the English administrative set-up. Universities that were established after 1835, strongly encouraged English as a language. English books, reports and other documentation were kept in the libraries and archives of universities. British rule regularised all levels of education, including higher education, in English. Soon, the British way started to become the only way.

English as a Language

The arrival of British ships on Indian shores brought along many reforms. Names of Indian scholars were replaced by English authors and poets like Shakespeare and Jane Austen. English was the common ground on which people from different regions came together and spoke one language. The British Raj strove to grab all intellects and bright students under one wing: English. As colonisation started, more and more establishments were built to facilitate the living of Englishmen. Thus, Christian schools and universities came about. Over time, discrimination became apparent between a British and Indian child. Indian students began prioritising the English language because the market demanded so. Getting a job under the English administration meant you had to be well-versed in English.

Education at the Regional Level

Ancient India was divided into provinces. In the year 1757, the East India Company took over the administration of India from the Mughals and established a government in Bengal, soon followed by Punjab, Bombay, Madras and Hyderabad. During this time, there were many changes to the governance of India and the provinces that made up the country. A number of these changes have been documented by historians over time.

Over time, every province had to follow the education system the British established in India. This included how they taught, what they taught, and what they did with the students after school. This was designed to perpetuate the colonial culture. The system was based on the English model of education. Even to this day, the education system in India is still largely influenced by the British colonial legacy and has been criticised for marginalising Indian culture and language. The curriculum is often too heavily focused on English, which has led to a decline in students' proficiency in other languages. Many Indians have called for a change in the education system so that it can better reflect Indian values and culture.

Women's Education

Until 1875, women were not allowed to seek admission to universities or get higher education degrees. But things started to change from 1882 onwards. Universities welcomed and encouraged women. The prejudices that segregated women from the rest of the world started to get washed away with the encouragement of women's education. It is a popular saying in India, 'If you educate a man, you educate an individual, but if you educate a woman, you educate a family (nation).' In the 1840s, Bombay province established the first-ever girl's school in India. Apart from co-education in universities, there were also English medium girls' colleges that were focused on creating an environment where girls were encouraged towards higher education. This exclusive set-up was solely to build an accessible and safe environment for women in British India.

Two movements influenced women's status—in the 1800s and early 1900s—the Social Reform Movement and the Nationalist Movement. Through these movements came significant changes in how society perceived women. Ram Mohan Roy, also known as the Father of the Indian Renaissance, was instrumental in abolishing the tradition of sati, where a widow due to customs burns herself on her husband's death pyre. A modernist, a social reformer and a man who challenged the evils of our society, Roy was also the driving force behind opposing child marriage and supporting widow remarriage. He also promoted women's education. During his lifetime, he instituted numerous reforms to improve the lives of widows and ended up fighting against forced marriages, polygamy, child marriages and the denial of property rights. He was a trailblazer in the fight against child marriage and the purdah system. On 4 December 1829, Governor-General Lord William Bentinck issued the Bengal Sati Regulation, which outlawed the practice of sati in all British Indian jurisdictions.

Iswarya Chandra Vidyasagar also advocated for women's rights, and his work resulted in the passing of the Widow Remarriage Act in 1856. Thousands of women took up these causes and fought back in a steadfast manner. Maharshi Karve was one of the individuals who backed them up in their fight. In 1912, he built SNDT Women's University in Maharashtra. In light of women's rights, women also spoke about their political rights which the leaders of India strongly supported.

The Emerging of Universities: 1857 to 1902

Indian universities have the authority to offer degrees and licences as they deem fit. Owing to the establishment of a higher education system in British-controlled India, many universities came up in different parts of the country. The Indian Universities (Honorary Degrees) Act gave three Indian universities the authority to award an honorary LLD degree. The Punjab University existed before 1857 but was re-established by an Act in 1882.

Private learning centres and institutions were built in great numbers between 1901 to 1921. During these twenty years, the political tensions in India rose due to the zeal for an independent India. The year after 1921 saw the emergence of many private institutions. It was the time when India desperately wanted its land in its own hands. No wonder, the number of educational establishments of the British Indian government could not keep up with the uprising of private colleges and institutions. Indians felt that to gain back social and political powers, education needed to be its backbone. Establishing its own colleges became a movement, and thus were born the Deccan Education Society of Poona and Mahamodan Anglo-Oriental College at Aligarh.

Table: Comparative position of Indian higher education in 1921–22

Management	*Number of Institutions*	*Number of Scholars*
Government	2,946	2,56,998
Board	53,188	30,72,412
Aided	93,629	35,01,766
Unaided	16,357	5,65,384
Unrecognised	16,322	4,22,165

The Hartog Committee of 1929

A report on the development of education in British India was submitted in 1929 by a committee called the Hartog Committee. Anything but advancement in educational growth would not satisfy the committee of the time. They were worried about the sluggish growth and wastefulness of elementary education, and they presented methods to mend this gap by focusing on literacy at various levels. The committee presented a report claiming that students were squandering money and denying themselves education by leaving school before finishing a certain level. The survey concluded that poor reading rates among school children had resulted in a dip in literacy skills. To address this problem, the report suggested taking a few steps: instead of expanding the number of schools, the government should pursue a consolidation strategy; the duration of the primary course to be four years fixed; teachers' quality, expertise, prestige, salary and working conditions needed improvements; adapting curriculum and instruction techniques to the living and learning environments of students in villages was crucial; local and seasonal needs had to be taken into account while determining school hours and vacations; and expanding the number of inspectors in the government institutions was the need of the hour.

Despite enormous expenditure on creation and execution, the matriculation examination in secondary schools resulted in a high number of failures. Early on, a lack of advancement from one class to another, along with a high degree of persecution from unqualified pupils, sought to squander the time and energy of busy professors. Rather than concentrating on just one subject, the course could be designed to cover a wide range of topics and fulfil the requirements of many pupils. The committee also recommended widening job pathways after middle school by allowing students to choose industrial or commercial careers. It also advised that university education and education for women and minorities be improved. The committee wrote a document outlining how the government should arrange volunteer education and assist the state in achieving educational stability. It was regarded as a crucial text in thoughtfully helping the reorganisation of the education policy of the time. The British East India Company's growth programme had failed, and when it tried a consolidation approach, it was in keeping with the Indian conditions of the time. Because of the 1930–31 economic slump, several of the committee's recommendations were unable to be implemented. The majority of their suggestions were only wishes.

Advancement of University Education (1921–37)

Between 1921 to 1937, there were great advancements in university education. The reasons for it were:

1. The framework of the Inter-University Board
2. Changes in the organisation of older affiliated universities (Bombay, Madras, Allahabad, Patna and Punjab)
3. Five additional universities being added to the mix (Nagpur, Delhi, Agra, Andhra and Annamalai)
4. More funding for research and military training
5. Physical activities and student housing were improved
6. Inter-collegiate and inter-university activities were expanded and developed.

Before independence in 1947, the period between 1921 and 1937 was the time when India was regaining its power. The freedom movement was at its peak. The Indian Congress worked hard to take back the leash in its hand. The vision of making India democratic and a republic was topmost in every mind. The granting of fundamental rights and freedom seemed near, and yet Indians had to keep up the fight for every inch of their land. The period can be called the last few years of British rule on Indian land – a rule that stretched from the mighty Himalayas to the lonely Andaman and Nicobar Islands. Even though the rule of the crown and the sceptre was slipping out of hands, the British tried their best to fix things and make a good impression of themselves. But not much could have been achieved when people were in the mood for a Non-cooperation Movement.

India is a land of diversity and the segregation of provinces is based on the culture of the group of people. Under British rule, people understood the concept of 'united we stand and divided we fall.' India started to revolt when all the provinces rose together. Amidst all the different cultural backgrounds, India united to get freedom. In such an environment, the universities thought that bringing together the courses and curriculum would be a great opportunity for similar higher education across the length and breadth of the country. Finding a common ground where all the students of India could study and learn in the same manner was crucial for the freedom struggle.

Bombay, Madras, Allahabad, Patna and Punjab were old universities. To decrease the load of older universities, new universities were established. They were Nagpur University, Delhi University, Agra University, Andhra University and Annamalai University. Private contributions were crucial to the establishment of these universities. For example, the Annamalai University in Madras was named after Raja Annamalai who initiated the establishment of the university by giving money to the Madras Government. Contributions continued for the research department, and more funding was provided for military training. Almost all great nations of the world were experiencing tensions among themselves at the time. Strengthening the military and recruiting more men into the armed force was a way of showing control in 1937 when the world was preparing for World War II. The Indian army was preparing to fight on behalf of British India.

As the new universities were being set up, it was important for the institutions to organise a place of residence for the students. The government stepped in here and participated in improving the quality of life of students by providing better places and environments to live in. Apart from education, physical activities were made part of the university curriculum. It certainly diversified the spectrum of learning. Moving out of the four walls of colleges, inter-college events and activities were encouraged. At such gatherings, students from different colleges met each other and shared their interests. Different sports and cultural activities took place which gave the students the chance to expand their horizons.

The Inter-University Board

Over time, it was realised that coordination amongst universities was very important and Calcutta University Commission emphasised it. When different universities came together in 1921, a proposal similar to the Calcutta University Commission was placed. At the same time, in England, the Lytton Committee also drew a similar stance on the recommendations. They wanted all Indian students across all universities to have coordinating courses, and the universities under the Empire to have a say regarding the higher education curriculum. To cement all these recommendations, Shimla hosted the first All-India Conference of Indian Universities, in 1924. Representations from all Indian universities took part in it. Since then, each year an annual meeting used to be held at a particular university to discuss the reforms and courses. Since 1925, the following were the workings of the board:

1. To serve as an inter-university organisation and information centre
2. To foster professorial interaction
3. To act as an authorised communication intermediary to make academic work easier to coordinate

4. To aid Indian institutions in gaining international recognition for their research, in terms of other countries' degrees, certificates and tests
5. To nominate or propose a common representative, as required, at national-level higher education conferences
6. To serve as an Indian university appointment bureau
7. To perform any additional tasks that may be given to it

The board did immense work to establish harmony and coordination among all the Indian universities. With the passing years, the work and functions of the Inter-University Board became stronger, and it became an integral part of the higher education system.

Inclusion of New Universities

On 21 February 1913, a Government Resolution on Educational Policy mandated that every province should have a university. It was the first step to providing a systematic higher education to the different provinces of British India. Each university stood as an affiliating body to support higher education establishments. These affiliations gave direction to the colleges. Five new universities came into existence after the education policy was passed. The first university was planned in Delhi, being the capital of British India. Delhi University was built in the province that was centrally administered, Delhi. After Delhi, a place in Maharashtra got the opportunity to build its first university: the Nagpur University, for Berar and other centrally administered provinces. Going down south, Madras saw the emergence of the Andhra University, largely to cater to Telugu-speaking people, to facilitate their higher education. Andhra University created curricula based on its mother language. In order to affiliate the universities for Gwalior, central India and the united province, Agra University came into existence. The capital of the Mughal Empire, Agra, is located on the banks of the river Yamuna, and houses one of the wonders in the world: the Taj Mahal. Last but not the least, a teaching university was formed in Chidambaram (Madras province) and was named in honour of its donor, Raja Annamalai Chettiar.

University of Calcutta

The University of Calcutta (CU) is a state university. Founded on 24 January 1857, it is Asia's first multidisciplinary, Western-style institution.

Ronald Ross, Rabindranath Tagore, C.V. Raman and Amartya Sen are the five Nobel laureates linked with this university.

Before India's Partition, the university was connected with 27 colleges in East Bengal (now Bangladesh). The Calcutta University Act of 1951, which replaced the earlier Act of 1904 and established a democratic structure for the university, was passed by the West Bengal government.

Delhi University

Delhi, the capital of both pre-Independence and post-Independence India, displayed the rules of the Crown as well as the sovereignty of the Constitution. Before the political leaders of India shook the British Empire, the scenario of the capital was different. The local conditions impacted the structure and foundation of the university. An act brought into being Delhi University, and the initial objective of the learning institution was to build a unitary residential and teaching university. Along with the strains from local conditions, lack of funds also stood as an important factor in front of the Hartog Committee. The Committee commented, 'It would be a loss to India if the healthy traditions of the three colleges were sacrificed by a too rigid adherence to the formula of a unitary university.'

The three colleges that were under Delhi University were St Stephen's College founded in 1881, Hindu College founded in 1899, and Ramjas College founded in 1917.

In 1927, a special committee was formed to discuss further the importance of building Delhi University and its functions. The then Government of India passed a few orders in the year 1934, clearly stating that a university following the federal type should be developed in Delhi. The following were the essentials required for a university of such type to finally come into existence:

1. There has to be close proximity between the university and its affiliated colleges.
2. Each college should keep up with the standards and work of the university.
3. Colleges have to cut off a fraction of their autonomy for the interest of the university and the government it is under. It would in return help the colleges to share and work with each other and form collaborations.

4. As far as possible, the college and the university should be the parent of the actual teachings and its curriculum.

Nagpur University

Nagpur is the winter capital of the state of Maharashtra and is also the third largest city in India. The government of the Central Provinces created a commission in 1914 to look into the possibility of constructing a provincial university in Nagpur. The report was received by the government in 1915, but preparations were put on hold. Amid a lot of struggles, the university was founded in 1919, and a board of trustees was constituted by the Act of Incorporation of 1923, to oversee its activities. This act established an affiliating university but nevertheless, it was written in such a way that the university may later grow its teaching side. With time, soon after the university was founded, it launched a Law College with the intention of turning it into a teaching institution as soon as possible. However, when poverty and other problems worsened, hope evaporated in 1937, and Nagpur University became primarily an affiliating university. It all started with great initiation but the government felt the heat of revolution in pre-Independent India.

Andhra University

The formation and expansion of Andhra University are of particular relevance because it was this new university that preceded the construction of a new province based on the same premise. Telugu was first spoken throughout a broad portion of the Madras Presidency, known as Telegu-speaking territories. After much debate, the Andhra University was incorporated into an Act of 1926 and given authority over the areas that made up the Madras Presidency, where Telugu is spoken by the majority of the native people. By adopting Section 3 of the Indian Language Learning and Teaching Act, the institution was looking for measures to encourage native Indian languages. The Arts College, which opened in 1931, and the College of Science and Technology, which opened in 1933, were the first two colleges established by the University of Andhra. Aside from these campuses, the institution also has affiliations with other colleges in the area.

Agra University

In 1927, Agra Institution was established as an affiliating university for universities with colleges that were much too controlled by an external university. It includes all of the provinces, central India, Rajputana and Gwalior. The university had a number of teaching organisations that deliver extension courses at its connected institutions. India had discovered a means to arrange university education despite its diverse culture, geography, and socio-political contexts. Other provinces were attempting to implement their own model after many institutions from various regions of India were united into one single university. It was done to establish as many teaching institutions as feasible in order to address the educational demands of Indian colleges.

Annamalai University

Raja Annamalai Chettiar did a gracious gesture by giving an endowment of 27 lakh rupees to the Government of Madras in the year 1926. In 1929, the Indian government created Annamalai University and gave it a grant of ten lakh rupees. They also increased the endowment fund by twenty-seven lakh rupees and made a one-time donation of seven lakh rupees. Students were separated into small groups and allocated to staff members. A tutorial system was also in place to guarantee that students receive enough advice and teaching. The university provided a variety of English and Tamil-taught disciplines, as well as research tools. To generate content for these courses, they collaborated with a research department.

Madras University

The University of Madras (also known as Madras University) is an Indian public state university located in Chennai, Tamil Nadu. It is one of India's oldest universities, founded in 1857 by an Act of the Legislative Council of India under the British government. In a public address to Lord John Elphinstone, Governor of Madras, 70,000 inhabitants signed the first such demand for higher education in the Madras Presidency. The university was organised in the model of London University. The University of Madras is the alma mater of two Nobel Laureates in Physics, C.V. Raman and Subrahmanyan Chandrasekhar, as well as other renowned mathematicians, including Srinivasa Ramanujan. The university currently has 121 affiliated colleges including prominent ones like Madras Christian

College (1837), one of Asia's oldest extant colleges, Loyola College (1925), and Stella Maris (1947).

Impact of British Rule on the Indian Higher Education System

Academic institutions and gurukuls in India were the lifeblood of education and tutoring for a vast portion of the local people. They attracted a large number of international students too. To meet colonial and political interests, Christian missionaries were employed to groom Indian people and make them suitable for the administrative tasks of the British government.

In the earlier periods of the British Raj, only the members of the Indian Royal families were given access to English education. The British feared that if ordinary people knew the English language, they might revolt against the government. In the twentieth century, however, Lord Curzon initiated English education among the masses. His efforts were a turning point in history, where the rulers were given autonomy of their states and they worked as agents to spread English education on their behalf. Holding architectural merit, many new universities were built during this period.

Patiala was the epicentre of the new flow of academics. In 1860 CE, the Maharaja of Patiala opened a school of languages, and degree colleges for medical and sports followed it.

English education began in the nineteenth century and grew into universities dedicated to educating future generations, similar to those in the United Kingdom. At that time, schools did not exist in the same way that they did in Europe. Higher education was still out of reach for many people. Indian institutions did not provide teaching facilities until the 1920s. India's education system was significantly less developed than that of other countries, with teaching centred on reading and writing and no technical training. Throughout the 19th century, women's education was neglected.

T.B. Macaulay, who served on the Supreme Council of India, was asked by the British to assist them in setting up an education system in India. He chose English as the medium of education and shifted funds intended for education to other sectors such as healthcare, infrastructure, and minor language development support. A new India was born in 1835, according to Trevelyan's *Life of Lord Macaulay*.

Root Causes Linked to Failure of British Governance

The British government took the responsibility for Indian education and issued many annual reviews to strengthen the foundation of the system. Apart from this, it also took to fix or amend certain aspects of technical or agricultural education. In the years before 1859, the revenue was mostly handled by the central government and the provincial governments hardly had a say in making changes to the education system. But the powers started to get distributed among provinces and it was led by Lord Mayo, in the year 1870. Between 1921 to 1937, the relationship between the Indian government and education saw troughs. The responsibility of the provincial government increased and the revenues had to be divided into different education departments. The shifts were not always smooth and the students had to adjust to many changes, especially because many youths were getting involved in protests, revolts and processions to make the country free.

English Education did not Come in Early

The East India Company did not regard the development of education for Indians as a duty or concern during its early years of government. Its principal goal, like all others, was monetary gain through commerce, and its early administrators neglected academics. But, like many other colonial countries in Africa and South America before them, they quickly grasped the need for education. Territorial gains were further in the character of capital investments than the establishment of the grounds of Imperial sovereignty, with growth, wealth and education of its subjects as its goal. The British had been in India for a long time before any type of education was developed for the Indian people. There was fierce antagonism to any system that favoured the British, who were seen as rulers by anybody who stood in their way.

Mr Wilberforce, a British philanthropist and politician, presented a new bill to add two courses to the 1833 charter for sending teachers to India. However, this idea was received with strong resistance by the Court of Proprietors, and it was determined that certain sections needed to be removed from consideration once more.

Racist Views and Remarks

The term 'brown people' was used to describe Indians, and they were subjected to unethical and immoral comments and the works that were loaded on the shoulders of Indians were too harsh. To succeed in getting on the side of the British, Indians had to sabotage their life and bow down their heads to foreigners in their land. The British government and the British society were not kind to Indians. They were treated as second-class citizens and had to live in a segregated society. The British government also passed laws that made it difficult for Indians to get jobs. Education was a far-fetched dream. The British East India Company was established in 1600 to trade in India. In the beginning, the company was successful but after 1757, it faced a lot of problems. British India is a period of time when the British were able to establish their power and policies in India. It can be argued that this period of time favoured the British. They divided people into different groups according to their religion, caste, ethnicity etc., which helped them maintain control over them. The British also favoured these divisions by creating new laws that would favour one group over another, for example, laws that would favour Hindus over Muslims or Brahmans over Untouchables.

The Education System favoured the British Administration

The education system in British India did not favour the Indian society. The British Administration had a lot of power over what they taught, how they taught it, and to whom they taught it. With such authority over the education system, they could easily shape what type of society Indians would have as well as keep them away from any ideas that could challenge their rule. The British administration in India during the colonial period had policies that favoured the British education system over Indian society. This was done to make sure that Indians were not able to overthrow the British rule in India by educating them. The policies were successful as they ensured that Indians were under-educated and unable to learn anything other than what they were taught by the colonial administrators and their appointed teachers. The British introduced English language education in 1835. The system was based on a one-size-fits-all model, with no allowance for cultural differences. This led to resentment among Indians and a sense of alienation from their traditions and culture. This led to the rise of a new generation of British Indians who were unable to write in their mother tongue as well as their native languages.

Not Following the Education Acts

Thomas Babington Macaulay was the very first person in Indian history to emphasise the importance of financial resources in education. Macaulay made a pivotal decision that altered the direction of education. In 1835, a British legislator and a legal member of the Council of India offered a critical minute that would forever alter educational systems. He spoke before the Committee of Public Instruction, basing his case on the key elements of the 1813 Charter Act. It is written in the Act, 'For the revival and promotion of literature and the encouragement of the learned natives of India, and for the introduction and promotion of a knowledge of the sciences among the inhabitants of the British territories.'

Macaulay defied the Legislature's rulings, which deprived him of his right to speak. Before 1835, the committee made key educational judgments, and individuals began to criticise them. They were not following the advice provided to them by the Parliament in their charter clause, according to Macaulay, and this resulted in a waste of resources. He stated that when the Parliament said 'literary', it meant Sanskrit literature or Arabic literature, but the committee emphasised on studying Locke's metaphysics, Milton's poetry, and Newton's physics. It opened the way for a trend of educational systems being changed in reaction to past initiatives. It is so uncanny that a British politician raised his voice against the Education Committee to change its route but it was too busy wrapping Indians with the covers of the British and unplugging the traditional education system in every way.

Other Issues

Health and Well-being

The British Indian government stifled innovation and research, despite the fact that early medical advances helped avoid epidemics. They lacked financial and other resources necessary to support their own inventive initiatives. In India, there was a time when medical research was not taken as seriously as it should have been. Aspects like preventative medicine were making a bigger effect and gaining a lot more traction. It took India over a century to accept medical research as a legitimate field of study. In 1884, the foundation stone for India's first medical laboratory was laid in Kasauli, near Shimla, which was a central lab. Provincial labs were vital components of public health, and were located in provincial capitals. Their mission was to provide facilities for testing, monitoring, analysis, and reference. In Kasauli, the Indian Pasteur Institute for Rabies Prevention was established in 1900. Similar institutes may now be found throughout India. In 1911, the Indian Study Fund Association was established to provide research grants on themes such as food. In 1918, the Nutritional Research Laboratory in Coonoor was established. In colonial India, the British Imperial government built a well-organised medical system, and it took the place of the traditional Indian and Arab medical systems. Early progress took a long time due to people's apathy about the process, as well as a lack of funds, health staff, and government backing.

The people of India were hesitant to embrace foreign services and occasionally opposed British colonisation. They were finally schooled in the British educational system. They, therefore made the decision to join the Indian military and civil services and participate in government matters in order to alleviate their problems. That is why the Indian Medical Services (IMS) of the late nineteenth and early twentieth centuries were so effective. In British India, medical and sanitary standards improved dramatically over the nineteenth century. IMS was able to effectively deal with diseases like the plague and cholera, thanks to steam-powered technologies. Smallpox, leprosy and malaria were all rampant during that period, but owing to IMS, they have all but disappeared. For many years, colonialism, narrow-minded policies, and neglect of indigenous peoples failed to alleviate the condition of Indians. Only after many plagues and influenza, public healthcare evolved since 1947.

Employment

The Zamindari system was prominent in India even before its colonisation. The zamindars used to give off small portions of land to harvest to landless farmers and cut off revenue after harvest. In another way, the zamindars used to allow peasants to work in their fields and pay them instead. The zamindars had to give revenues to the British Empire in return. When the crop was bad, the peasants had to face harsh conditions and debt from the zamindars. It led to many farmers taking their own lives. The administration and other government services had jobs for Indians. That being said, there was no other great infrastructure to hold up the weight of India's population. Thus, many people had to sustain on business or work at small local firms.

Contributions to the Development

Few people and historians have made remarks on India's past by concluding that India would have still remained savage if the British did not bring modernisation along with them. India was ahead of its time from ancient times and the land had its own saga of aiding life in many ways. The perception of many Western people to call India a savage country is completely distorted. The advancement of medical science in India as well as education was advanced from the beginning. The diversity, lifestyle and languages of the land were subject to ridicule during colonisation. In a recent interview, S. Jaishankar, Minister of External Affairs mentioned that the British took away 45 billion dollars of today's worth from India. In addition, Indian troops were exploited by the British to fight World War II on their behalf. It caused a lot of people to migrate and settle in other countries. The developments done in India were only to ease the works of the British Empire, including the building of railways and the Indian Postal Service. There were no specific things done keeping the interest of Indians in mind.

THREE

Education
A Privilege for Independent India

Education is the most powerful weapon which you can use to change the world.

– Nelson Mandela

Students' Involvement in Independence

India's Independence was a tough fight at all levels. Although not everyone became freedom fighters, almost all were passively linked to the revolt to throw the British out of their land. At the heart of this revolt were many college and university students who participated in and supported the different protests and processions for freedom by Indian leaders. The Indian National Congress (INC) brought many passionate and patriotic members under its wing. On the other hand, the party also saw Netaji Subhash Chandra Bose leave the INC and form his own army. While Mahatma Gandhi preached the motto of non-violence and said, 'If someone slaps you on one side of your face, turn the other one to him,' Netaji was an extremist and he delivered, 'You give me blood, I will give you freedom.' Their approach to freedom and independence was entirely different but regardless, it attracted millions of people on both sides.

The Swadeshi Movement (a self-sufficiency movement to encourage the use of Indian goods and to boycott foreign-made goods) drew a large part of the society as active participants. This was successful because Indians could no longer bear the British exploiting them with harsh laws and assaults. College students were a major part of the Independence movement and raised their voices against the British. Women came out of their houses and heavily participated in picketing and processions. *Hartals* (closure of offices and shops in protest) disrupted the functioning of the British Empire, and many students disturbed court proceedings by smashing windows and pelting police with pebbles and stones. The idea of bringing about change and forming a new India proliferated political discussions in universities, libraries, bars and many more public places. These discussions included printing presses, nationalistic views, circulating pamphlets, politics, collection of funds, arrangement of political meetings and others. However, the Government of Madras came out with harsh policies banning students from attending political meetings because they were afraid that the rise of patriotism among students would have a huge impact.

Non-Cooperation Movement

The Non-Cooperation Movement, also known as the Indian Independence Movement, was a campaign of civil disobedience launched in 1920 by Mohandas Karamchand Gandhi. Its goal was to end British rule in India through non-violent means. It was an era of political awakening among not only the leaders but also the university students. Goods produced by the British were boycotted. Men and women started wearing clothes that were manufactured by local Indians. Khadi, homespun cotton, became the norm. The movement also saw many students quitting government educational institutions. Open-air meetings witnessed the footfall of students and women. It is estimated that around 90,000 students left their government colleges and universities to stand with nationalistic views. Dropping out of college did not mean that they halted their studies. Instead, they pursued their higher education in more than 800 national schools that were not under the British Indian Government. The Indian city that the East India Company first set foot on, Calcutta, saw the most effective educational boycott among students. The Swadeshi Movement spread to Punjab and then also to Assam, Bombay and Uttar Pradesh. National educational institutions dumped the British education system and brought Indian ways to talk about the damages that the colonisation did. Additionally, those institutions trained young men and women to develop the non-colonisation framework. Students, teachers of national colleges, inmates of Gandhian ashrams and Khadi Bhandar workers were the strong backbone of the disobedience movement.

Aligarh Muslim University, Aligarh

The revolt of 1857 changed the perception of Sir Syed Ahmad Khan and it made him understand that through modern science and the English language, the Muslim community could make a forward stance in the movement of change in India. The Muslims in India were a remote community and were in desperate need of quality education. Sir Syed was a staunch supporter of social change and a prominent national figure in India. He started schools that specialised in diverse disciplines to provide the groundwork for a Muslim university. In 1863, he had the notion of establishing a scientific institution to provide better scientific education among Muslims and to provide Indians with access to Western-born knowledge in their local language. Sir Syed's goal was not just to establish a college, but also to disseminate Muslim-managed schools throughout the country. Given the success and growing number of Muslims, he established the All-India Muslim Educational Conference (AIMEC) to assist and advocate their cause on a national level. This led to the establishment of the Aligarh Muslim University (AMU), which, over time, became an educational force to reckon with. AMU continues to attract a large number of foreign students from all around the country and the world.

University College of Science, Technology and Agriculture, Calcutta

Sir Ashutosh Mukherjee was the pioneer behind one of the oldest and most well-acclaimed universities in India. Back then, he was the vice-chancellor of the university and Sir Taraknath Palit and Sir Rashbehari Ghosh made generous donations for the prospects of the university. Acharya Prafulla Chandra Ray, Sisir Kumar Mitra and Chandra Sekher Venkata Raman were among the first faculty members to join the institution. The batch of 1915 is still known as a legendary batch as it constituted intellectuals like Satyendranath Bose, Jnanchandra Ghosh, Meghnad Saha and Jnanendranath Mukherjee. Calcutta University's research was not a colonial endeavour because it received no imperial assistance and benefited little from imperial resources.

Laxminarayan Institute of Technology, Nagpur

The Laxminarayan Institute of Technology was founded in 1942, because of the generous contribution of D. Laxminarayan. He was aware of a lack of technological expertise in the province and wanted to address the gap. Because he was among the forward thinkers of his time, his work came into contact with challenges that only technologists could solve. His objective was to assist others in making a difference, while also making the entire society progressive. A plan was developed in 1934 to launch a two-year BSc (Tech) programme. Harisingh Gour chose the institute's current location in 1936. In 1937, the university selected Ram Simha Thakur as an Officer on Special Duty to monitor the project's development till completion. The institute was dedicated to providing high-quality education as well as conducting research and development to satisfy the demands of the chemical processing industries. Under the rules of the Maharashtra Public Universities Act, the institute, as a university-governed and controlled college of RTM Nagpur University, is responsible to all of its surrounding stakeholders, including pupils, employees, faculty, alumni and industries.

Dandi March

The Dandi March is a great example of how individuals can make a difference in the world by uniting with other members of society. It also shows how one person can make an impact on society and change it for the better. The Dandi March was a protest organised by Mahatma Gandhi in 1930. It was a march of several thousand Indians to the seashore in the village of Dandi, Navsari district in Gujarat, to break the monopoly on salt held by colonial British India. Gandhi started the procession with only 78 people but the strength of the procession increased to about three kilometres. This small group and Gandhi went to different villages to inspire and give speeches. Gandhi garnered young students as part of his procession and they walked with him to the very end of Dandi. His message of *Satyagraha* (holding onto the truth), a route to non-violence, influenced many university students to join the campaign of the Civil Disobedience Movement.

Azad Hind Fauj (Free Indian Army)

Netaji Subhas Chandra Bose stands as a tall icon of someone who fought with the vision of driving away from the British and made allies with countries like Japan, Burma, Germany and others. 'The enemy of my enemy is my friend' was the notion that led Netaji to shake hands with the notorious tyrant, Hitler. Azad Hind Fauj led by Netaji was the reason for many mutinies in the British Indian Army. Netaji's speech and drive to show India a better day caused the nationalism in many British Indian troops to revolt. The formation of INA (Indian National Army) also known as Azad Hind Fauj gave the British government a tough time, as the INA troops of more than 62,000 soldiers fought for their motherland. The daring approach of Netaji and INA reverberates in the hearts of youths to this day. Pranab Mukherjee, former President of India, conveyed to the Netaji Research Bureau, Kolkata, 'On this historic occasion, I pay tribute to Netaji Subhas Chandra Bose and urge the youth of India to adopt the slogan of *Itmad* (Faith), *Ittefaq* (Unity) and *Kurbani* (Sacrifice) which Netaji gave to the soldiers and civilian personnel of the Azad Hind Fauj.'

The Dawn of Freedom and Rights

When India finally broke its shackles from the British Crown and gained its freedom, Jawaharlal Nehru said, 'At the stroke of the midnight hour, when the world sleeps, India will awake to life and freedom. A moment comes, which comes but rarely in history, when we step out from the old to the new, when an age ends, and when the soul of a nation, long suppressed, finds utterance.'

His words continue to ring in the ears of Indians. Raising flag of India and proudly singing the national anthem drew a lot of sacrifices from the people of the land. In the year of Independence, in 1947, India had abundant human resources of 340 million. When the British descended on the sacred land of India, the literacy rate was alarmingly low. Only 12 per cent of Indians were literate, and the percentage of people who had completed their higher education was even lower.

A lot of resources and services were sucked out of India before the land gained Independence. The boundaries of pre-independent India and post-independent India were markedly different. Syed Ahmed Khan, a pragmatic Indian Muslim, presented the two-nation theory, and thereafter India was divided into two nations: Pakistan and India. The former became a Muslim country and the latter took on the secular word and added it to the Preamble of the Constitution. The Radcliffe Line divided the nation into two, and around 14.5 million people crossed the line. The governments of both nations failed to deal with such a huge mass migration, and it led to violence on both sides. Historians estimate that hundreds of thousands died due to the division of India. This migration uprooted people from their hometowns and placed them in refugee camps.

The Crown of the Mainland and of the State

Jammu & Kashmir and Ladakh are now two union territories of the former state of Jammu and Kashmir (J&K). Before the division, the state, which is home to the Himalayas, was called the Crown of India. But India remembers that it was not easy to pull up the crown as it was the tail of the upper neighbouring country and truth be told, a beautiful tail. The crown also hid a lion and his small pride and their militia stood as a major reason for the last Dogra monarch to give away Jammu and Kashmir to India. Now one must wonder how does higher education impact all this.

In Kashmir, Sheikh Mohammad Abdullah is known as the lion. He belonged to the Kashmiri Muslim community who even though were educated, were still marginalised. Sheikh Abdullah came across discrimination on the grounds of education but he managed to become the first Kashmiri Muslim to obtain a Master's degree in Chemistry. He wanted to pursue a doctoral degree in Chemistry in England, and applied to the J&K government for the same. But his application for a grant was rejected. By that time, liberal and progressive ideologies took over the Sheikh and he was convinced that the feudal system was the one to blame for the inequality among the Kashmiri people. In the year 1931, Sheikh Mohammad Abdullah revolted along with other people against the king of the state, Hari Singh.

Hari Singh really wanted J&K to remain an independent kingdom. But the turn of political events made him seek help from the Dominion of India. In exchange for support from Indian troops, Hari Singh had to accede to India. It is said that if Kashmiri Muslims were given equal opportunities as the Hindu elites, they wouldn't have revolted. During the 1947 partition, there were only over 2,000 educational institutions in J&K, and they were funded by only 7 per cent of J&K's revenue. Small steps were taken towards improving the educational conditions and in the following year 1948, the University of Kashmir was established, along with a Textbook Advisory Board. Hari Singh remained the king of J&K until 1952 when the Indian government abolished the monarchy.

Education—A Distant Dream to an Average Citizen

During the nationalist movements to free India, one of the main objectives was to make the youth of India patriotic. However, when the Nehru government was finally established after independence, it failed to adopt any effective educational policy. The reason being that education was not the immediate focus; the economy was. India was in desperate need to stand on its own feet as decades of exploitation had left it with nothing. Revival needed time and the country needed immediate nutrition. In 1941, Rabindranath Tagore said, 'The wheels of fate will someday compel the English to give up their Indian Empire. What kind of India will they leave behind, what stark misery? When the stream of their centuries' administration runs dry at last, what a waste of mud and filth will they leave behind them?'

By the time the British were completely out of Indian territory, India was one of the poorest countries in the world. As the British fought World War II, India was drained of its resources and Indian troops were sent to fight on behalf of Britain. The Great Bengal Famine that cost India three million people was man-made because Churchill wanted to feed his English soldiers rather than the people who fought for him. Apart from this, another major challenge was that the entire structure of the economy, infrastructure and bureaucracy included, was designed to very well suit the interests of Britain, not India. Additionally, the British ensured the partition of the Indian subcontinent led to millions of people being killed. With such massive setbacks, India was left stark naked and hungry. It is recorded that by the time India got its independence, half of its citizens were below the poverty line. It shows that there was certainly no room for people to fill their heads before they filled their stomachs. To continue studies or even opt for studies, financial and mental stability were needed, which were not something Indians could afford. Bearing the burden of more than 80 per cent of the population being illiterate, the Nehru government established the first Education Commissions in 1948 and 1952. For the next two decades, the government only focused on the evolution and general development of education. The enactment of the Indian Constitution made India a democratic country and along with it, it was the first step towards educational development.

Untouchability was a social evil, and even though the Indian Constitution gave equal rights to all its citizens, this was a harsh reality for the lower castes. For students who belonged to poor households, pursuing higher education was a distant dream as the setup of primary education was not approachable by many. The stigma of belonging to lower castes, the fear and shame made people from these sections of society curl up into their shells and survive on the leftovers of the upper caste people.

Gaining independence was not enough to change the circumstances; changing the mindsets of people and making equality real to the entire nation was the need of the hour.

National Institutions Set Up under the Nehru Government

Nehru said, 'Science has no frontiers. Nobody ought to talk about English science, French science, American science, or Chinese science. Science is something bigger than countries.'

The developmental blueprint by Jawaharlal Nehru had two folds. At first, he wanted to replicate world-class institutions in India. By the time Nehru became the first prime minister of India, America was booming with the advancement in science and technology. During his visit to America, Nehru decided to replicate the same in India. His visit to the Massachusetts Institute of Technology (MIT) in 1949 put ideas into his mind to create similar institutions in India. Thus, it gave rise to the Institutes of Technology in Kharagpur (1950), Bombay (1958), Madras (1959), Kanpur (1959) and Delhi (1961). All of these establishments were publicly supported to ensure that a lack of money would never prevent Indians from receiving the highest education possible.

IIT Kharagpur

IIT was established in 1946 with the purpose of fostering post-war industrial growth. The goal was to give high-quality education and generate scientists and engineers with practical skills, so that India could become more industrialised. In its report, the 22-member committee led by N.R. Sarkar, in a study, proposed the implementation of four higher technology institutions in the eastern, western, northern and southern regions, possibly modelled after the Massachusetts Institute of Technology in the United States, with a number of secondary institutions affiliated with it. The study also called for the creation of four new institutions as soon as possible to replace the ineffective ones in the east and west. The commission's goals were to develop undergraduate students who were capable of doing research, creating art, and teaching professionally. The assumption was that these students would meet or exceed the standards set by other disciplines. The concept behind '2×1' numbers was that enrolling twice as many undergraduates as graduate students would provide the department with additional hiring and class scheduling flexibility. Indian Institute of Technology was founded in 1950 in Hijli,

Kharagpur, on the proposal of the Sarkar Committee. The IIT was first established at 5, Esplanade East, Calcutta, and was quickly relocated to Hijli in September 1950. On 18 August 1951, it changed its name from Eastern Higher Technical Institute to the Indian Institute of Technology. The college was born and raised in the former Hijli Detention Camp, where freedom fighters worked and died for the country's liberation. The Kharagpur Institute of Technology, or IIT as it is more often known, has very few ties to jails. In truth, it was founded about the same time when the Kharagpur Detention Camp was converted into a security and justice facility. Reforms can sometimes take place on the other side of the world. With 224 pupils and 42 professors, the inaugural session began in August 1951. The Hijli Detention Camp's historic structure held instructional rooms, labs and administrative offices. With only 11 departments, the institute began its academic programme. Pandit Nehru laid the foundation stone for the new building in March 1952.

All the buildings on the current campus were planned by Dr Moser, who also directed many of the projects in partnership with a number of engineers and architects. Many historic monuments in the United States have his signature, demonstrating his international influence on architecture. The Ministry of Industry and Supply provided substantial financial assistance for the purchase of a number of machine tools. The Institute Workshop aspired to be one of the country's best. Sir J.C. Ghosh was the institute's first director, and under his direction, the institute was able to build a magnificent foundation from which it could continue to flourish into its current shape. Dr B.C. Roy presided over the inaugural governing board, which included prominent people like Sir Jehangir J. Gandhi, Mr N.R. Sarkar, Mr H. Kabir, Dr Tarachand, Mr T. Sivasankar, Mr K.R.K. Menon, Dr S.S. Bhatnagar and Dr J.C. Ghosh. The institute had prominent scientists like Prof. R.A. Kraus and Prof. H. Tischner as early as its formative years, and they were the first two heads of the Electronics and ECE departments. The Indian Institute of Technology (Kharagpur) Act was approved by the Indian Parliament on 15 September 1956, designating this institute as a national institution. In 1950, the IIT was elevated to the status of a university, and it continued to grow and expand at a steady pace. There are now 18 academic departments and five research institutes on campus. The campus spans over 2,000 acres and is densely forested with trees and structures. On the lot, there are over 5,000 individuals, including roughly 1,700 academic members and around 900 pupils.

IIT Bombay

IIT Bombay was established in 1958, and has remained an important element of the Indian education sector ever since. The IITs were designated as institutes of national importance by the Indian Parliament, in 1961. The Government of India organised a committee to nominate four higher colleges of technology to guide India's technical growth. The first class of hundred students was enrolled in 1958 after planning began in 1957. The institute had grown to encompass approximately 500 academic buildings on six campuses, totalling over two square kilometres of ground space, as well as around 170 teaching centres. UNESCO created IIT Bombay in 1958, and the Soviet Union provided funding for its creation. UNESCO offered a wide array of equipment and technical specialists, while the Indian government agreed to bear the majority of the costs, including the construction costs. Powai, an industrial and residential district in Mumbai, was chosen as the location for the institute. In 1967, the Bombay government donated the land for the institute's construction. While construction was underway, the institute's first academic session began on 25 July 1958, with 100 students at the Synthetic and Art Silk Mills Research Association (SASMIRA) facility in Worli.

These students were chosen from over 3,400 applicants for first-year engineering programmes in Chemical, Aerospace, Civil, Computer, Physics, Electrical, Engineering Energy, Metallurgical Engineering, Mechanical, and MSc Chemistry. One of the institute's key goals was to create facilities for research in a variety of specialised engineering and technology disciplines. It was critical to develop suitable facilities for postgraduate study and research. While the institute was temporarily located at Worli, an effort was made to speed up its development, and Jawaharlal Nehru laid the foundation stone for its permanent home. The Ministry of Human Resources and Development, along with five other Indian institutes, bestowed the Institute of Eminence designation upon IIT Bombay on 9 July 2018. With this prize, it was able to make a greater influence on Indian education and have access to more money.

IIT Madras

IIT Madras is one of India's most prestigious technological universities. These national institutes provide young students from all over the country with world-class engineering education. The institute is located in south Chennai, on a 630 acres campus that houses over 3,000 students. It also includes faculty and staff personnel, as well as their families. For years, the IIT has been a world-class success story, and it continues to position itself as a leading research, consulting and technology development centre. West Germany's government provided India with a better alternative than its own nation in terms of assisting in establishing a technology institute. This caused Nehru to think about it for a long time before accepting their offer. In 1959, in Bonn, the first Indo-German agreement was struck to construct the Indian Institute of Technology in Madras. The Indo-German agreement permitted the utilisation of German academics and other instructors, as well as the training of twenty Indians. In addition, a central workshop was built to provide a variety of scientific and technological equipment. Prof. Humayun Kabir, Union Minister for Scientific and Cultural Affairs, formally opened the institute in 1959. Dr A. Lakshmanaswamy was appointed as the inaugural chairman of the board of governors, and Dr B. Sengupto was appointed as the director at the time.

The Indo-German Technical Assistance Programme began in 1962, with the visit of Dr Heinrich Lubke, President of the Federal Republic of Germany. Since then, the institution has benefited from close cooperation that has helped develop it. The Industrial Consultancy Centre was established in 1973 by Shri C. Subramaniam, Minister of Industry and Science. In the same year, the institute received IBM System/370 Model 155 computers. Inter-university collaborations in R&D and industry consulting, post-graduate training in television engineering, and a variety of other ventures between Germany and India began in 1974. The Employees' Welfare Scheme was established in 1975 to assist with the financial burden of workplace accidents. Evening DIIT courses were established in 1983 for engineers who live or work in Chennai. France's aerospace industries became more competitive, thanks to a 1976 agreement with the French government for collaboration and aid in a key French sub-industry. The Indo-German partnership was extended for another five years, with more multifaceted initiatives and international activities. The lab was improved to the point that it could now generate new breakthroughs to benefit from. In 1979, the credit system for evaluating university degrees was created.

IIT Kanpur

The year IIT Madras was established was the same year as IIT Kanpur too was established. The Indian Institute of Technology, Kanpur, was founded in 1959 and is one of India's finest educational institutes. The institute's mission is to deliver meaningful education, undertake high-quality original research, and give technical innovation leadership. The Kanpur Indo-American Programme at IIT Kanpur not only allowed students to keep up with advances outside of India, but it also allowed them to keep up with their scientific colleagues. It was primarily concerned with staying ahead of the curve and adjusting as necessary. From 1962 until 1972, the Kanpur Institute in India got technical help from a group of nine American universities. These universities were UCB, MIT, California Institute of Technology, Ohio State University, Carnegie Institute of Technology, Princeton University, University of Michigan, Case Institute of Technology and Purdue University. The university began with the Kanpur Indo-American Programme, which established labs and curricula. The institute's first director, P.K. Kelkar (1905–2002), was recognised in 2002 when the central library was renamed the P.K. Kelkar Library. IIT Kanpur became India's first institute to provide computer science instruction in 1963, under the direction of economist John Kenneth Galbraith. IBM machines powered the first computers used for education in India, which ran on the system from 1963 to 1967. Prof. H.K. Kesavan, who was chairman of Electrical Engineering and head of the Computer Centre at the same time, was the one who developed computer education. Harry Huskey assisted with computer activities at IIT Kanpur prior to the establishment of their Computer Science and Engineering department in 1971. The institute started a separate academic programme in Computer Science and Engineering in 1971, which led to M.Tech and PhD degrees. Owing to tensions surrounding the United States' backing for Pakistan, as well as diminished government financing due to a drop in pupils wanting to study engineering at the Indian Institutes of Technology, the KIAP programme stopped in 1972. Techkriti, the institute's yearly technical festival, was founded in 1995. IIT Kanpur is a 420-hectare campus located along the Grand Trunk Road in Uttar Pradesh, roughly fifteen kilometres from Kanpur's centre. The government gave this property in 1960, and the institute moved there in March 1963. The institute has more than 6,000 students, including around 4,000 undergraduates, 2,500 postgraduates, and 500 research associates.

IIT Delhi

Established in 1961, the College of Engineering was renamed the Indian Institute of Technology (IIT) Delhi in 1997. It was designated as an institution of national importance under the Institutes of Technology Act, 1963. The government then designated it as a deemed university, giving them the authority to set their own policies and administer exams for degrees. IIT Delhi has around 48,000 graduates from diverse fields, leaving many competent and talented people after graduation. These figures indicate the statistics of Ph.D. and B.Tech. students who completed their degrees in 2014. Nearly 5,070 students graduated with a Ph.D. out of around 16,000 students with a B.Tech. This professional engineering school's graduates have master's degrees in a variety of subjects, which they utilise to work as scientists, technologists, business managers and entrepreneurs today. Alumni from the institutions who work in administration, politics or non-governmental organisations have contributed significantly to the development of our country. They've also had a significant influence on the industry. Several alumni have gone on to other fields of expertise and have made significant contributions in the previous several years to help improve this country, workplaces and industries. Dr Sircar founded the Indian Institute of Technology (IIT) in 1950 as a method to provide education to a wider audience and make it more accessible to people across the country. IITs sprang up all around India during the following few years. The Sircar Committee advised that similar institutes be established around the country to offer secure and healthy learning environments for those interested. The government adopted the Sircar Committee's proposals, which included the establishment of further technical institutes with the assistance of friendly nations. India has a long history of partnership with the Soviet Union, including a UNESCO agreement that established the first IIT. Following that, three Institutes of Technology with cooperation from West Germany were founded in Bombay, Delhi and Madras.

Were the Replicas Suitable for the Indian Society?

Many political leaders who were leading the country forward were influenced by their English education. The India of 75 years ago was completely different than what it is now, naturally. It desperately needed freedom, and the liberty to live in an open and liberated environment.

Creating replicas of foreign institutions did not help improve the skills of Indians. The education policies were focused on uplifting minorities, the backward castes and women, and increasing approachability. The awakening of free India needed such measures but more could have been done in the education field. It was as if even though India had driven out the British, it was still holding on to colonial habits. American history is different from Indian history and the traditional values of our educational roots should have been more highlighted. Back then, the education system took the intellectuals and filled the seats of national institutions and discarded the rest on many levels. India was abundant in human resources, thus filling up vacant seats was never a problem. But what about the students that did not have proper guidance to pursue higher education? India was steeped in poverty, and pursuing higher education was not possible for most of the population. Human resources were turned into mechanical bodies, often not providing nourishment to their brains. Many torchbearers have debated the huge population of India and its disadvantages. The more people in poverty, the more stress the government pulls in. The economical division in the then-Indian society had to be lowered and the huge difference between the economically higher people and those below the poverty line needed to be highlighted.

India jumped into replicating international universities and taking help from developed countries for establishing those. The education system failed to uplift the skills of the population and make them ready for the international market. The weaker students of the system had no programmes or proper guidance and the students from rural areas were hit the most. The cloud of darkness did not let the light of knowledge into the huts of rural areas. *Gram Panchayats* (village-governing institutes) were formed in all villages, but the availability of affordable quality education was lacking in every corner of the country. Girl children were forced to get married at a very early age, and the boys were handed farming tools instead of pencils and papers. Although the knowledge of farming or other works got transferred from one generation to the other, the people needed more modernity to increase their efficiency. As the world progressed, technology and science played a huge role in it. India somehow got left behind, owing to many factors.

Table: Dropout Rates at Primary, Elementary and Secondary Stages of Education

Classes I–V	*1960–61*	*1970–71*	*1980–81*
Boys	61.7	64.5	56.2
Girls	70.9	70.9	62.5
Total	64.9	67.0	58.7
Classes I–VIII	*1960–61*	*1970–71*	*1980–81*
Boys	75.0	74.6	68.0
Girls	85.0	83.4	79.4
Total	78.3	77.9	72.7
Classes I–XII	*1960–61*	*1970–71*	*1980–81*
Boys	NA	NA	79.8
Girls	NA	NA	86.6
Total	NA	NA	82.5

The Non-Parity of Languages

The Constitution of India stood as an important rule book and the change was quasi-static at the beginning. A British framework could never understand or uplift the lives of Indians. The British template of higher education was continuing to push English as the main language. The spectacular and diverse languages of India were seen as unwanted ones. Even though the British left, Indians never scraped off their system which was very much needed. Making strong modifications and moulding the system to suit its citizens was much needed. After the parity of English, Hindi became the official language of India. Many people were opposed to it, and anti-Hindi agitations took place in Tamil Nadu. Many south Indian senior leaders resigned to protest against the motion. To break the monotony of exhaustive debates, Hindi was made the official language for a period of fifteen years, in 1950. But the next fifteen years were not enough to cool down the aspirations and wants of non-Hindi speakers. In 1965, the Indian government made efforts to continue the usage of Hindi as the official language but had to face criticism and harsh comments.

With days passing by, the anti-Hindi movement gained momentum with the help of college students. Dravidian people wanted English to be the official language of the country but the Indian government was firmly against it. College students were agitated enough to join the movement and a riot broke out on 25 January 1965. The then Prime Minister Lal Bahadur Shashtri assured that both Hindi and English would be used as official languages, to calm down the situation. During the Indira Gandhi government in 1967, the Official Languages Act was amended to reinstate the usage of English and Hindi as the official languages.

Slow but Steady Developments

The National Department of Education was under the Ministry of Human Resource Development. The Central Advisory Board of Education would give advice to both government ministries on educational matters. The Ministry of Home Affairs is responsible for internal security and law enforcement in the country. India has a number of intelligence agencies. The Research and Analysis Wing has been the primary intelligence agency specifically tasked with monitoring domestic threats, foreign intelligence and terrorist activities in India. The National Investigative Agency was to be responsible for investigating organised crime, terrorism and financial offences involving corruption. Thus, maintaining harmony both inside the country and outside was essential. Independence was followed by many regional riots mostly tainting the heads of college students. Political parties used the youth in their favour to raise their voice for their agendas. The period of teenage and early adulthood takes a human being through a lot of changes. During such phases, the outburst of emotions is not mature. Political parties used this to their advantage.

The Department of Education had several autonomous organisations: the All-India Council of Technical Education (1945), which regulated technical education and other academic matters; the University Grants Commission (1953), which regulated financial assistance and admission processes at universities, as well as degree-awarding and governance; and the National Council. The National Council of Educational Research and Training (NCERT), which is the nodal agency for all educational matters in India, was created in 1958. It is the main department responsible for organising, running and governing schools, colleges and universities in the Department of Education. There are various autonomous organisations under the council's purview, such as the All-India Council of Technical Education. The first body advises the government on technological education to fulfil its responsibility to maintain standards with regard to further development. There are also organisations that have the responsibility of managing particular parts of the country. For example, the Central Water and Power Research Station (CWPRS) is a research institution that was established in 1916 to carry out research on water and power. This is one of the many organisations under the council's purview, such as Punjab Agricultural University. The second organisation, the University Grants Commission, was charged with promoting and coordinating university education, as well as maintaining teaching and examination standards. They may also handle any financial concerns that arise at the university. The Ministry of Human Development works to enhance India's educational standards. It collaborates with other government agencies on policies and significant initiatives, as well as with students to provide healthy learning environments.

The central government operated and provided schools for the children of their own employees as well as those of employed government employees. These schools have a focus on academics, but they also accept students who are qualified regardless of whether they can afford it or not; these are the ones seen as high achievers. Public schools are open to any student who is qualified and can meet the enrolment requirements. In general, public schools have lower tuition fees than private institutions. For the first time, India set up a plan for decentralised education to be implemented across each state in the country. The Kendriya Vidyalaya Sangathan was founded on 15 December 1963.

The issue of quality of education has been plaguing the country since time immemorial. Over the years, there has been a drastic decline in this area. The reason is that the state of education varies significantly from state to state and quality is not uniform across schools.

India's educational institutions grew significantly during the mid-20th century. The country boasted of more than three times as many colleges and universities by the 1980s. In the 1990s, India's college-age population boomed and universities were bustling with degree batches. Non-formal and adult education systems were improved or expanded by the government. As the world gets more technologically advanced, it is becoming increasingly vital for everyone to have an education.

The Damages from Naxalism

Naxalism had been a hot topic of discussion in the Indian state of West Bengal. It was a political and militant movement that aimed to overthrow the Indian government by using armed struggle. The Naxalite movement has been active in India since 1967. The movement spread rapidly, and its influence was felt not only in West Bengal but also in other parts of India such as Bihar, Andhra Pradesh, Tamil Nadu, Punjab, Maharashtra and Kerala. Naxalism is an ideology that advocates violent revolution to overthrow capitalist society and establish a communist society based on common ownership of land. The Naxalite movement is one of the most significant social movements in the history of modern India. It was founded by Charu Majumdar on 15 August 1967 at Naxalbari, West Bengal. The movement began as a peasant rebellion against feudal landlords, moneylenders, and the exploitation of tenant farmers by landowners. Naxals believe that their struggle is for liberation from exploitation and oppression, which they see as being perpetuated by capitalists rooted in Indian society. They see themselves as part of a worldwide revolutionary struggle against capitalism and imperialism. They also see themselves as part of an internationalist struggle to end poverty. Naxalism is a key issue that has been plaguing the country for decades. The Naxals have been fighting against the government and its policies, which they believe are detrimental to the rights of people living in rural areas. They have also been involved with several social movements, such as women's rights and caste struggles. The way college students got involved in Naxalism has been widely researched, but there are still many questions about why students joined this particular cause and what their motivations were for joining.

On 9 April 2009, a 16-year-old student commented after his school was brutally damaged by the Naxalites: 'This school has been badly damaged... The whole building has been ruined, the windows are smashed and blown, and the floor is cracked, as are the walls and the ceiling. Even the door is broken. The wall outside that connects to the veranda is also destroyed, everything is in ruins.'

Despite assertions to the contrary, Human Rights Watch research shows that both Naxalite assaults and government occupations may make it difficult for children to get an education. In India, for example, Naxalite attacks became more common in later years, resulting in the closure or destruction of several schools and educational institutions. Government jobs have also resulted in an increase in insecurity in the regions where they exist.

While the central government along with state governments had taken stricter actions to sabotage the spread of Naxalism, the year

1971 in Calcutta was in turmoil. Political assassinations became more widespread in Bengal over time, and the government at the time was powerless to stop them. Extremist attacks, as well as right-wing violence, escalated. Soon after, a political solution developed on its own. The Naxals, or members of the Naxalite movement, encouraged young adults to join them. College Street and the surrounding area, which housed Calcutta University and over a dozen other institutions, were constantly a hive of activity. Students would rush around preparing for India's long-awaited revolution. The state government not just had to deal with the Naxalites, but they also had enormous pressure from the national government, which was led by Indira Gandhi and embodied by West Bengal's Siddhartha Shankar Ray. As a gesture of goodwill, the government freed prominent Naxalite leaders from prison in 1969. This backfired, and all the diverse left factions banded together to establish the Communist Party of India (Marxist-Leninist) to continue their revolutionary struggle.

In the year 1975, when the fifth president of India was Fakhruddin Ali Ahmed, he declared an emergency due to internal disturbances. A large number of youths were killed in encounters during that time. Many parents lost their young sons to the bullets of policemen and the military.

Such active militant movements affected students in a big way. Many senior leaders of such groups target college students to make them a part of the revolution by brainwashing them according to the ideologies of the group. Naxalites have been against a capitalist mindset. For them, the government should not be taking land from farmers and turning it into land for the production of infrastructure. Naxalites became the third-wheeler between the government and the public. Many universities became the storehouse of political agendas. Marches, protests, processions and *bandhs* (a day when offices, shops, schools and other places close for the day and citizens stop working to express their displeasure about something) were very much exercised on the campuses and outside. Many ex-students of Calcutta colleges like Presidency College remember the way slogans were chanted on the campuses, to spread the Naxal ideology.

Implications of the Industrial Revolution

According to studies, higher education has a positive relationship with industrialisation and vice versa, and such results are scientifically supported. Industrialisation is related to invention and benefits humankind in many ways. It is difficult to identify the beginning of the industrial revolution, but by looking at the early indications of the utilisation of machinery, one can say that the Agrarian Revolution was the first indication of any kind of change. Global industrialisation ushered in a period of fast industrial development in the 20th century, resulting in the emergence of technologically-driven sectors.

Throughout history, higher education institutions have taken various shapes. The great universities of Takshashila (Taxila) and Nalanda are two examples from the ancient world. Buddhist monasteries have existed from the beginning of recorded history, yet it's impossible to determine when they first appeared and what their true origins were. Higher education in Takshashila was mostly centred on literature and science. Buddhist and non-Buddhist disciplines could be studied in Nalanda. We now live in a world where unanticipated societal shifts are occurring continuously. People are increasingly recognising the significance of globalising in order to expand social spaces and foster cross-cultural understanding. Fishery, farming and animal husbandry are subjects taught in many universities now.

The Correlation in India

Higher education is increasingly being viewed as a long-term investment rather than merely a means of obtaining a job. This implies that universities are important not just for providing students with the professional opportunities they desire, but also for the development of any economy. India is making rapid progress in meeting the demands of its young in order to expand its workforce and keep the economy afloat. From first-generation students to internationally recognised institutions, India's higher education system bears the weight of a massive and varied population. The history of colonialism has varied through time and locales, with various policies being implemented in reaction to criticism. Even while it was successful in removing many biases, it nevertheless created disparities and made the colonised feel inferior. As a result, certain portions of this history are not what they appear to be, allowing for change and reconstruction. With a history of colonialism and a booming service and industrial sector, India's economy is certainly moving towards improvement.

Table: India's rate of growth for GDP

Year	*GDP Growth Rate of India*
1960	5.5
1970	5.2
1980	3.6
1985	4.8
1990	5.6
1995	7.3
2000	5.8
2005	9.0
2006	9.5
2007	9.9
2008	6.1
2009	6.7
2010	10.0

Universities Set up by Indian Philanthropists

A philanthropy-based university is a university that is funded by private donors or foundations, rather than government support. They are often affiliated with a large corporation and have the goal of creating a degree that will be useful in the workforce. These universities have also become popular because they are more affordable than traditional colleges as they do not have to spend as much on infrastructure or academic buildings. The benefits of philanthropic universities are many. They provide a space for students to be socially engaged, contribute to the community and also offer career opportunities for graduates. In India, a new breed of charitable higher education institutions has emerged in recent years, and they appear to be in tune with our generation's expanding expectations. However, due to a lack of precise and trustworthy information and data, distinguishing between for-profit and non-profit organisations may be difficult. The true markers of the philanthropic nature of an institution may be the track record of sponsors in the care sector, rational fee structure, natural order of programmes on offer, scholarship programmes to deserving students from disadvantaged sections of society, and advancement of scholarships on long-term social issues. While philanthropy in higher education is more difficult than many people believe, the concept of trusteeship may have merit.

These new institutions have the potential to create a culture of understanding and care, which would need organisations to invest in their employees. This could also mean organisations invest in an employee's career path while promoting collaboration among colleagues. and motivating employees to feel valued. As organisations adapt, there could be a shift in the values of potential employers toward focusing on team cohesion and objective truth. By this, it means that the institutions will help shape a culture where employees are encouraged to build relationships and trust with each other outside of work. This shift might make people feel less threatened by their colleagues' knowledge. The system is also a great place to experiment with different courses and see what the students like. This can help students decide their career paths and establish a plan that meets their current needs. The courses are designed in such a way as to let students learn at their own pace. Institutions are trying to create a friendly and fair space on their campuses where students can pursue their academic goals without the interference of vested interests or manoeuvring experienced by many of the state-run public universities. In order to do this, they are trying to develop and apply a set of shared standards for evaluating student work. They do not just abandon our traditional models of evaluation, but rather innovate in their process. These institutions have something valuable to contribute and it reverberates among the students.

Indian Institute for Science

The Tata Indian Institute of Science (IISc) is a public, deemed research university dedicated to science, engineering, design and management instruction and research. Established in Bangalore, the capital of Karnataka, the institute was founded in 1909 with the help of Jamsetji Tata. It is one of India's most prominent academic institutions, with the highest number of citations per professor. After an accidental meeting between Jamsetji Tata and Swami Vivekananda on a ship in 1893, Tata wrote to Vivekananda five years later to thank him: 'I trust, you remember me as a fellow traveller on your voyage from Japan to Chicago. I very much recall at this moment your views on the growth of the ascetic spirit in India... I recall these ideas in connection with my scheme of Research Institute of Science for India, of which you have doubtless heard or read.'

Tata was intrigued by Vivekananda's views on science and leadership ability. Tata intended to improve India's scientific capacity, and Vivekananda was enthused about the initiative. To accomplish so, he formed a provisional committee to assist in the establishment of a research and higher education institute. On 31 December 1898, the group provided Lord Curzon with a draft proposal. The Nobel Laureate Sir William Ramsay was then asked to suggest a suitable location for such an institution. Bangalore was identified as the ideal place. The Viceroy, Lord Minto, sanctioned the institute in 1909. To make it work, a requisite Vesting Order had to be signed. The Maharaja of Mysore laid the foundation stone for this institute in 1911, and the first students were admitted to the departments of General & Applied Chemistry and Electro-Technology on 24 July 1911, under Norman Rudolf and Alfred Hay. The Department of Organic Chemistry was established in 1958 and received declared university status from the University Grants Commission two months later.

The Evolution of Higher Education

Independence Era

The burden of colonialism fell heavily on higher education. The British Raj had a significant impact on higher education in India. This is due to the perception of universities as deserted and abandoned institutions. The universities in India before independence were mostly funded by the British government and the curriculum was designed to serve their interests.

Post-Independence Era

Nehru's strong socialist leanings defined the decade after independence, probably due to the Soviet Union's considerable power. The objective was to use centralised planning to promote industrialisation. The state put a lot of money into higher education in the high-tech field to make this happen. The process of increasing capacity required a lot of effort, but it was well worth it.

Between the 1970s to 80s

The 1970s and 1980s were defined by a harsh socio-democratic agenda that was distinctly protectionist. Individuals in the post-Nehru period were less concerned with professional education. They believed that state investment in higher education was not as spectacular as it had been in the past and that they would have to rely on social welfare approaches rather than caste-based institutions in the future. The requirements of skill development, on the other hand, remained a significant goal pursued by a variety of measures, while the emphasis was on a policy-based response to the needs of skills training rather than on content. Public-private partnerships, educational loans and subsidies were all examples of this. As a necessary consequence of the above-mentioned distancing from globalisation, the country experienced an economic downturn that bordered on a crisis. The growing trend of insularity is a significant worldwide phenomenon. Higher education is no exception, which implies that in order for students to profit from their education, courses and learning have to be globalised. Later, India seized the opportunity and revolutionised according to the way the world educates its children. Humanities and social sciences occupations declined dramatically while engineering and technology jobs increased. If students wanted to keep up with the changing employment market, they needed to learn a new skill set.

FOUR

Reforms of Independent India

A Resource-constrained Long Battle Towards Literacy

I measure the progress of a community by the degree of progress, which women have achieved.

– Dr B.R. Ambedkar

Education in Growing India

The diversity of India—with its many languages, peoples and cultures—can confuse anyone! Many people from the West think of India as an unregulated and chaotic country. The lack of a thorough educational infrastructure only adds to this image. The previous governments have always stressed on education, but not enough.

India needed time to heal from foreign invaders, plunderers, British colonisation, the partition and more. Along with time, many things have improved, and a lot more needs to be done, including achieving political stability. India needs a strong leader who can be a powerful representative of the nation and can uphold the tenets of democracy, apart from ensuring overall development that includes a solid educational infrastructure that is accessible to all. Since independence, not much has been done for education until in recent years.

The Suppression of the Traditional Educational System

The rich land of India which was ahead of the rest of the world was taken advantage of, due to lack of a proper administration. The policy of *Atithi Devo Bhava* (Guests are like Gods) cost India heavily, as it welcomed invaders and colonisers, innocently believing them to be well-wishers. After gaining independence, the educational infrastructure slowly started to take shape. 75 years into independence, we must take this opportunity to understand that knowledge and education are different. Even though independent India lacked modern skills and equipment, it still held in-depth knowledge. The Vedas and other ancient scriptures unravel vital lessons of life; lessons that have been seasoned from ancient times.

In many parts of India, people still rely on the goodness of Ayurveda and Yoga. The modern world is co-existing with traditional wisdom. Many doctors are turning to Ayurveda to find and formulate medicines with no side effects. Ancient Indian wisdom has holistically taken care of the physical body as well as the mind and soul as ancient India was the birthplace of spirituality. Slowly, lessons under the open sky were replaced with teaching sessions inside four walls. English was brought to India only for the sake of the British, and for the recruitment of Indians to work in the British Indian administration. Whether this foreign education system was transformative for Indians, remains debatable.

The National Educational Policy

The National Educational Policy in India was introduced in 1968. It is a document that lays down the guidelines for the development of the education system in India. The policy is based on the principles of equity, access to quality education, and social justice. The policy has been revised twice, once in 1986 and then again in 1992. The 1986 revision was to incorporate recommendations from the National Policy on Education 1986 and to take into account changes that had taken place since 1968. The 1992 revision was made to bring about changes that were needed because of advances made in technology and other developments since 1986. The National Educational Policy has a vision of achieving complete development and integration of all aspects of a human being through education. The need for a new policy arose because India has changed drastically since 1986. The population has grown exponentially, there are more children to educate with fewer resources available, and there are many more demands on education due to globalisation.

India's independence put the spotlight on the alarming illiteracy rate, and since then programmes were set up to counter the situation. The discussions were not only regarding rural areas but also urban areas. A series of commissions were set up to come up with proposals and build a modern system of education in India. Maulana Abul Kalam Azad, the first education minister of India, and also one of the most influential

Muslim leaders in modern India, envisioned a powerful centralised and standardised educational system. His role in the struggle for India's independence from British rule was immense. He was born on 11 November 1888 in Mecca, Saudi Arabia, to a Bengali Muslim family. He had his early education in India and then went to Al-Azhar University, Cairo, for higher studies and obtained a degree in Arabic literature. He returned to India in 1910 and joined the Indian National Congress in Lucknow in 1916. Azad is also remembered as one of the most influential and powerful orators of his time, with a unique style which combined Western oratory with Eastern cultural references, and Islamic symbolism. This influence on his education led the Union government to form the University Education Commission (1948–49) and then the Secondary Education Commission (1952–53). It was continued with the establishment of the University Grants Commission, and then the Kothari Commission (1964–66) to make recommendations regarding the education system.

NEP 1968

There was no National Education Policy (NEP) under the government of Jawaharlal Nehru. But when his daughter, Indira Gandhi, became the first female prime minister of the country, she introduced the policy within two years of her into the prime minister's office.

Indira Gandhi's administration issued the first National Policy on Education in 1968, based on the recommendations of the Kothari Commission. The study advocated for comprehensive change and equitable educational opportunities. Through cultural variety, it aimed to foster national integration and progress. The policy calls for compulsory schooling for all children up to the age of 14, as specified by the Indian Constitution. Educators should get specific training and certification in order to lead and manage schools. The policy is intended to safeguard children from exploitation, abuse and prejudice, as well as to advocate for higher-quality education and to guarantee that instructors are certified. It was founded on the principle of increasing societal engagement. The move would increase education quality in India by offering equal opportunity to all students throughout the country. The policy also advised that schools should adopt the three-language formula where Hindi, India's official language, be part of the medium in all courses. Furthermore, the strategy called for the teaching of regional languages alongside English in schools.

It argued for the teaching of three languages: Hindi, English, and the official language of the state in which the school was located. Language instruction was regarded as critical for closing the intellectual-mass divide. Language, as vital as it was, was only the beginning. Underneath this was a whole educational system. This comprised a curriculum and a science of education to ensure that children truly understood how to utilise their language. As a result, while the language programme may be considered as a normal by-product of colonisation, it also needed to be given its unique identity. Hindi was the most widely used language in India, and many people advocated for it to be designated as the country's official language. Regrettably, this has also led to disputes or strife. The strategy promotes universal learning in order to let Indians, regardless of background, interact with one another and speak one common language. The teaching of Sanskrit, India's ancient language, was one of the beneficial aspects of the 1968 Education Policy. The government spent six percent of its GDP to educate pupils on a nationwide scale.

NEP 1986

The Indian government's National Policy on Education, which was implemented in 1986, emphasised the significance of eradicating inequities and working for equality. Part of these efforts were aimed at educating Indian women, who were previously barred from attending school and were occasionally denied an education. The enactment of this educational statute boosted the number of females attending school while also addressing gender disparities in education. These policy impacts were especially visible in places where female literacy rates climbed faster than male literacy rates, like Bihar, Uttar Pradesh and Rajasthan. To safeguard female children, India passed the Child Marriage Act in 1978, which barred marriage before the age of 18. The strategy advocated for more scholarships, adult education, more instructors from the SCs, and incentives for poor families to take their children to school on a regular basis in order to establish a more socially integrated society. It also advocated for the creation of new institutions and the provision of incentives for people to integrate into the mainstream. The doctrine encompassed reforms to education, science and technology, and liberal democracy. It intended to establish new institutions that would promote peace, development and democratic government. According to the doctrine, the government should provide incentives for persons who were unable to assimilate into the mainstream due to economic restrictions. The National Education Policy pushed for a child-centric approach in primary education and started Operation Blackboard to reduce disparities in primary schools across the country. The strategy aided in the development of the open university system, which provided degree courses through the Indira Gandhi National Open University, an organisation dedicated to providing higher education to children in India. The policy was also founded on Mahatma Gandhi's worldview. The ministry advocated for a rural university paradigm to foster economic growth in rural India. The education department intended to spend 6 per cent of the GDP on universities and schools.

NEP 1992 (Modification of NEP 1986)

The P.V. Narasimha Rao government revised the 1986 National Policy on Education in 1992. Former Prime Minister Manmohan Singh implemented a new strategy in 2005, based on his United Progressive Alliance (UPA) government's 'Common Minimum Programme', which is still in effect today. The primary education policy goal is to ensure universal access to basic education by combining public and private resources. The initiative also intends to lower dropout rates and raise literacy rates. The government intends to do this by extending possibilities for children aged 6 to 14, with a focus on girls, and guaranteeing that all pupils complete primary school. Furthermore, the National Policy on Education 1986 included a Programme of Action (PoA) 1992 that called for the administration of a national entrance test to admit students to graduate and postgraduate programmes. The Indian government established a three-tier admissions system for engineering and architecture/planning programmes. The Joint Entrance Examination (JEE) is the highest tier, followed by the All-India Engineering Entrance Examination (AIEEE) at the national level and, ultimately, an examination at the state level. Using these programmes allows for the preservation of various entrance requirements as well as the maintenance of high professional standards. This also eliminates overlapping concerns and lessens the physical, mental, and financial stress on children and their parents.

Encountering Caste System and Creating Reservations

From ancient times, Indian society was divided into four parts—Brahmins, Kshatriyas, Vaishyas and Shudras. In Indian mythology, the God Brahma is the creator of the universe. At the top of the Indian hierarchy are Brahmans born from the head of Brahma, and these are the teachers and intellectual beings. To protect land and territory, there are the Kshatriyas. They are known to be the warriors who took birth from Brahma's arms. The next in line are the Vaishyas and they are the traders. It is believed that from the thighs of Brahma took birth the traders. Lastly, there are the Shudras who are supposed to do menial jobs and are believed to be born from the feet of Brahma. The caste system in India is complex. The four castes are further divided into 3,000 castes and 2,500 sub-castes.

Despite the fact that caste has existed in Hindu society for generations, it has risen to prominence only in the last century. According to historians, official caste divisions were of little importance to Indians until the eighteenth century, when social identities were much more fluid and people could easily switch from one caste to another.

According to studies, British colonial rulers erected stiff barriers when they utilised censuses to simplify the system and create a single community under their common law. Many people were unable to escape the harsh social orders that had been in place for decades as a result of this. Given the struggles, some Dalits, and other lower-caste Indians have achieved significant positions. The Maharaja of Mysore, a well-known royal in modern India, was a Dalit as well. B.R. Ambedkar, the author of India's Constitution, and K.R. Narayanan, the father of modern Indian economics, were from this caste. Ambedkar was one of the most prominent Indian politicians, philosophers and economists of the 20th century. His views on social equality and justice are well-known among the Indian population. He was born on 14 April 1891 in Mhow, Madhya Pradesh, in conditions of socio-economic discrimination, in the Mahar family to Ramji Maloji Sakpal, a subedar in the British army and Bhimabai Murbadkar Sakpal who was from Maharashtra. He was educated at local schools such as Bombay Scottish School and Elphinstone High School where he excelled academically as well as athletically, playing cricket and football for his school teams. In 1904, Ambedkar passed his matriculation examination with high marks which gave him access to study at Elphinstone. Ambedkar and other untouchable children were separated from their peers in school and received little attention or assistance from teachers. They were not allowed to sit as equals in class. When they needed water, someone from a higher caste had to pour it from a great height because they were not allowed to touch the water or the vessel that held it. This chore was usually completed by the school peon for the young Ambedkar, and if the peon was unavailable, he had to go without water. Later, in his writings, Ambedkar described the situation as 'No peon, no Water'. He had to sit on a gunny sack that he had to carry from home.

Dr Ambedkar thought that these social issues had an impact on politics. He advocated for a proportionate share of political power based on population size. Socio-economic democracy is the only method to develop democracy for the poor, as it delivers policies that address their social issues, was Ambedkar's philosophy. He thought that India could not be really free of exploitation unless its most vulnerable inhabitants' rights were respected. With this in mind, Gandhi spearheaded the Indian Independence movement in order to empower such neglected communities for India to thrive and attain real freedom. Because Congress did not strive truly to promote the interests of the oppressed classes, Ambedkar believed that a separate battle for independence with a methodology and strategy distinct from the Congress was required. The philosophy of pragmatism is Ambedkar's philosophy. Political democracy is about gaining power, but social democracy is about empowering society. Ambedkar aspired to enter politics not for political dominance, but for social empowerment. Thus, Ambedkar led India's independence war using the middle way as a tactic and democracy as an ideal. Ambedkar's battle for Indian freedom has a social as well as a political message.

Ambedkar attended three Round Table Conferences (RTCs) in London as a Dalit delegate: the first RTC ran from 12 November 1930 to 19 January 1931. The second conference happened from 7 September 1931 to 1 December 1931, and the last meeting was held from 17 November 1932 to 6 February 1933. B.R. Ambedkar emphasised the need of engaging with opponents, whereas Congress believed in boycotting the opponent. However, seeing the futility of this tactic, Congress dispatched Mahatma Gandhi to the second Round Table Conference only to resist Dalits having separate electorates. Gandhi agreed to give distinct electorates to Indian Christians, Muslims, Europeans, Sikhs and Anglo-Indians, but he did not believe in giving separate electorates to Dalits. Finally, on 24 September 1932, Ambedkar and Congress leaders signed the Poona Pact. This resulted in joint electorates as well as an increase in reserved seats, which were later incorporated into the Government of India Act. Dr Ambedkar was continually seeking new ways to advocate for Dalit rights, and he worked with opponents on the matter. On 1 May

1932, Nehru sent a message requesting that Dalits be recognised as a distinct group of people, distinct from other oppressed classes such as the Backward Classes.

Dr Ambedkar founded the Independent Labour Party on 15 August 1936, with the intention of engaging Dalit politicians in debates about workers, labourers and peasants. Dr Ambedkar believed that it was critical to create a platform for their opinions in opposition to the British administration. On 7 November 1938, he staged a demonstration and, in 1939, he confronted the British by proposing fresh concepts about federation vs. freedom. Ambedkar notably advocated for the establishment of Pakistan. The Hindus and Muslims belonged to two separate civilisations that are so different from each other that neither appears to be worth comparing with the other. Ambedkar realised that in order to organise the labourers from these lower castes, he would have to first try to coordinate their jobs such that they all worked for the same enterprise. As a result, he established the Dalit Federation, an organisation of lower-caste labourers. Later on, quotas were expanded in 1989 to accommodate the Other Backward Classes (OBCs), who fall between the upper and lower castes. With the rise of secular education and increased urbanisation in recent decades, caste has lost some of its power, particularly in cities where multiple castes coexist and inter-caste marriages are becoming more widespread. Following social reform efforts in many southern and northern Indian states, individuals began using only one name. Caste identities stayed strong despite this transition. Last names, in particular, have long been used to identify caste.

Dr Ambedkar was a pivotal player in India's movement for independence, and he played an important role during this critical moment in Indian history. He provided the newly independent country with a new path to take. When he was elected to the Constituent Assembly on 3 August 1947, he was designated as the first law minister of independent India. Ambedkar was also the head of the Indian Constitution Committee, which began writing the Constitution on 19 August 1947. His drafted Constitution for India was ratified on 26 November 1950, called Constitution Day, and took effect on 26 January 1951. One of the most distinguishing elements of the Indian Constitution is its emphasis on social equality and justice for all of its residents. Because of his devotion to his country's unity and integrity, Ambedkar rose from an ordinary person to a renowned leader. He never considered the British or Gandhi's Congress as adversaries, but rather as competitors. To combat Britain or to diverge from Gandhi and Congress, he chose a very distinctive tactic. His policy of 'No boycott, but interaction with an opponent' carved a place for Ambedkar in the annals of India's freedom struggle. Ambedkar's socio-political ideas are acknowledged throughout the political spectrum in post-Independence India. He was a firm believer in individual liberty and an outspoken critic of caste-based society. Through socio-economic and legal incentives, his ideas have influenced all aspects of life and revolutionised the way India views socio-economic policies, education and affirmative action today.

University Grants Commission

The University Grants Commission is a statutory body set up by the Government of India to regulate and supervise the universities in India. It was inaugurated on 28 December 1953. The UGC is responsible for maintaining standards of higher education and ensuring that there are enough institutions to meet the country's needs for qualified personnel. UGC does not have any regulatory powers over the universities and their affiliated colleges, but it can only give suggestions for improvement in their regulations. It has been given the responsibility to take care of all matters related to university education, research and development in India. The commission also provides financial assistance for the construction and maintenance of buildings at universities and colleges, grants scholarships for meritorious students from low-income families, and monitors standards of teaching at universities. As the Ministry of Human Resources Department was changed to the Ministry of Education, therefore UGC is under the latter now.

The present structure of the education system goes back to colonial times. It focused on the importance of teaching European sciences and the English language. In 1835, when Lord Macaulay put forward his Minutes, it said, 'efforts to make natives of the country thoroughly good English scholars.' Sir Charles Wood's Dispatch of 1854, also known as Magna Carta of English Education in India, suggested forming a proper eloquent scheme of education that covered primary education to the university level. The government adopted a policy to promote indigenous peoples' education. Following that, the universities of Bombay, Calcutta and Madras were established in 1857, with Allahabad following in 1887. The Inter-University Board was founded in the 1920s to facilitate information sharing and cooperation among institutions. It enables collaboration in education, culture, sports and other sectors. Later on, the board was called the Association of Indian Universities. The report of the Central Advisory Board of Education on Post War Educational Development in India, better known as the Sargent Report, was the first effort to establish an Indian educational system in 1944. It was suggested that a University Grants Committee be established. In 1947, this committee was tasked with making choices about the work of three major universities.

Following the independence of India, the University Education Commission was established in 1948, with Dr S. Radhakrishnan as its chairman, to report on Indian university education and suggest improvements and extensions that might be desirable to suit the present and future needs and aspirations of the country. It was therefore proposed that the University Grants Committee be reorganised in accordance with the overall organisation of the University Grants Commission in the United Kingdom, with a full-time chairman and other members recruited from among educational authorities famous for their dependability. In 1952, the Union Government (of India) determined that any requests for grants from public funds to be allocated to central universities or other universities and institutions of higher learning might be forwarded to the University Grants Commission. As a consequence, on 28 December 1953, Maulana Abul Kalam Azad, the then minister of education, Natural Resources, and Scientific Research, formally inaugurated the University Grants Commission. The UGC was formally constituted as a statutory agency for the coordination of university education standards in India by an Act of Parliament in November 1956. The UGC recognised that India is big and varied, thus it established six regional offices to ensure that all areas receive equal attention.

UGC Mandate

- Promoting and coordinating university education.
- Serving as a critical link between the Union and state governments, as well as educational institutions.
- Creating regulations governing basic educational criteria.
- Developing and sustaining university standards for teaching, examination and research.
- Monitoring improvements in collegiate and university education; making funds for universities and colleges.

- Advising the federal and state governments on the steps that must be taken to strengthen university education.

Central Universities

A central university is a publicly funded institution of higher education in India, designed to mass-produce degree holders. The central universities can be thought of as the leading ivies of India and have a centuries-old history in either producing scholars or delivering high-quality teaching throughout India. In India, central universities are public educational institutions. They are formed by an Act of Parliament and are under the jurisdiction of the Ministry of Education's Department of Higher Education. In general, universities in India are accredited by the UGC as well as the 15 various specialised councils that provide students with a specialised learning experience. So far, 16 separate universities have been founded, as governed by the Central Universities Act of 2009.

State Universities

It is common in India for state universities to be run and funded by the state government of each of its states. In addition, the University Grants Commission is a central agency of the Government of India which gives financial support to state universities. To receive a grant from the government, state universities are required to put up an annual report on their budget and expenditure, stating what they have spent on research and development over the past years.

Deemed Universities

Deemed universities are the educational institutes in India that have been given the status of a university by the University Grants Commission of India. The UGC has established criteria for granting deemed university status to an institute. The institute must meet all the criteria before it can be granted deemed university status. There are both private and public universities in India's higher education system. Public colleges are funded by the federal and state governments, whereas private institutions are frequently supported financially by other groups. The position of a deemed university gives for total freedom in terms of courses, curriculum, admissions and fees. These institutes have self-government authority and are recognised by the UGC. There were 126 deemed universities in India as of November 2020.

Education Ministers

An education minister has the power to make decisions about school and university curricula, standards of teaching, and even what books are taught in the classes. In India, an education minister is responsible for overseeing the country's overall education system.

Table: Chronological order of India's Education Ministers – from independence till date

S. No.	*Name of Education Ministers*	*Tenure*	*Duration*	*Past Works/About*
1.	Maulana Abul Kalam Azad	15 August 1947 – 22 January 1958	10 years and 5 months	He is the first Education Minister after the independence of India and to date has the longest tenure. The ministry, under his leadership, established the first IIT in 1951 and UGC in 1953. In his honour, his birthday is celebrated as National Education Day in India.
2.	Dr K.L. Shrimali	22 January 1958 – 31 August 1963	5 years and 6 months	He served as an editor to a monthly magazine called *Jan Shikshan*. As a Minister of State, for his contributions to Indian education, he received the Padma Vibhushan in 1976.
3.	Shri Humayun Kabir	1 September 1963 – 21 November 1963	3 months	Under the first Prime Minister of India Jawaharlal Nehru, he served as the third Education Minister for three months. He was born in Bangladesh but later on completed his higher education at Calcutta University.
4.	Shri M.C. Chagla	21 November 1963 – 13 November 1966	2 years and 11 months	Under the Nehru government, he became the Education Minister and was devastated by the quality of Indian education. He stated, 'Our Constitution's fathers did

S. No.	*Name of Education Ministers*	*Tenure*	*Duration*	*Past Works/About*
				not intend that we just set up hovels, put students there, give untrained teachers, give them bad textbooks, no playgrounds, and say, we have complied with Article 45 and primary education is expanding. They meant that real education should be given to our children between the ages of 6 and 14.'
5.	Shri Fakhruddin Ali Ahmed	14 November 1966 – 13 March 1967	5 months	His unfortunate death while still in office has been given screen time in a short documentary film. He was the second Muslim President of free India and is known to announce an Emergency at midnight in 1975, after a meeting with then-Prime Minister Indira Gandhi. Apart from education, he also served different portfolios of the Central Cabinet like Cooperation, Industrial Development, Company Laws and Food & Agriculture.
6.	Dr Triguna Sen	16 March 1967 –14 February 1969	1 year and 5 months	He is the first Vice-Chancellor of the famous university in Kolkata named Jadavpur University. In the year 1965, he was given the Padma Bhushan. From 1967 to 1974, he was an active member of the Rajya Sabha and also became the 11th Vice-Chancellor of Banaras Hindu University.
7.	Dr V.K.R.V. Rao	14 February 1969 – 18 March 1971	2 years and 2 months	He was associated with many notable conferences, and committees and learned

S. No.	*Name of Education Ministers*	*Tenure*	*Duration*	*Past Works/About*
				bodies across the globe. His contributions to high-quality economics education and research in India were praised by former Prime Minister Manmohan Singh. Nationally and internationally, he has been the central force for the establishment of many universities. He held an array of publications and also formed an autonomous public body called the Indian Council of Social Science Research.
8.	Shri Siddhartha Shankar Ray	18 March 1971 – 20 March 1972	1 year	To the then Prime Minister Indira Gandhi he proposed to inflict an internal Emergency and prepared a letter to the President requesting that the declaration be issued, and demonstrated to her how democratic freedom might be curtailed while being within the bounds of the Constitution. Thus, he played a great role in the Emergency between 1975 to 1977.
9.	Prof. S. Nurul Hasan	24 March 1972 – 24 March 1977	5 years	As Minister of State, he had a significant influence on raising the number of teachers in India who are part of a career promotion programme that allows them to remain politically impartial. He was a driving force behind the adoption of 10+2+3 education systems, which are presently regarded as one of the top types of education available in India. He assisted in the

S. No.	*Name of Education Ministers*	*Tenure*	*Duration*	*Past Works/About*
				presentation of one of the first comprehensive studies on women in Indian history, which was submitted by a commission formed by the Government of India. He was also the driving force behind the establishment of 27 social scientific research institutes in India. During his tenure as a minister, the Rampur Raza Library was entrusted to the Government of India by an act of Parliament for financing and control. He was Vice President of the Council of Scientific and Industrial Research (CSIR) in New Delhi from 1977 to 1980.
10.	Prof. Pratap Chandra Chunder	26 March 1977 – 28 July 1979	2 years and 4 months	Between 1961 and 1968, he worked as an attorney in the Calcutta High Court, as a Supreme Court lawyer, and as a law professor at Calcutta University. Chunder was a powerful character in Indian history who worked in a variety of capacities. He joined India's ruling INC party in 1962 and served as Education and Social Welfare Minister from 1977 to 1979. Chunder was the Founder-Chairman of the West Bengal Heritage Commission and the President of India's first MBA school's board of governors. He served on the university's executive council from 2000 until 2005. From 1989–90

S. No.	*Name of Education Ministers*	*Tenure*	*Duration*	*Past Works/About*
				until 1993–94, and again in 1998–99, he served as President of the Presidency College Alumni Association.
11.	Dr Karan Singh	30 July 1979 – 14 January 1980	6 months	He is the son of Hari Singh, the last ruler of Jammu and Kashmir. Under the government of Charan Singh, he served as the Education Minister. To become the youngest member of the Union Cabinet, he resigned as Governor of Jammu and Kashmir and held portfolios like Tourism and Civil Aviation between the years 1967 and 1973. In 1971, he was a Union Cabinet Minister when the then government abolished official symbols, privileges, titles and remuneration of all princely states. He donated his remuneration to a charitable trust and stood in favour of the motion.
12.	Shri B. Shankaranand	14 January 1980 – 17 October 1980	10 months	He was a Cabinet Minister under eminent Prime Ministers Indira Gandhi, Rajiv Gandhi and P.V. Narasimha Rao. For 29 years, he represented Chikkodi in the Lok Sabha constituency. He won seven times from the same place consecutively, making a record.
13.	Shri S.B. Chavan	17 October 1980 – 8 August 1981	11 months	He earned his Bachelor's degree in arts from Madras University and his LL.B. from Osmania University. He began his legal career as an advocate.

S. No.	*Name of Education Ministers*	*Tenure*	*Duration*	*Past Works/About*
				During the Quit Court Movement in the old Hyderabad state, he founded the Students' Movement and ceased practising law.
14.	Smt. Sheila Kaul	10 August 1981 – 31 December 1984	3 years and 6 months	She was India's oldest living Member of Parliament at the time of her death. She had previously served as a leader in the Indian National Congress, as a Cabinet Minister, and as Governor, as well as in several social democratic battles for justice for everyone. In the State of Uttar Pradesh, she was also an educator, social worker and social reformer. During British India, she was an independence campaigner.
15.	Shri K.C. Pant	31 December 1984 – 25 September 1985	9 months	He had been a part of a large educational reform movement since the 1980s. He was able to develop key programmes such as Education for the Blind, the Mass Literacy Campaign, and Education for All, which enabled students to have more chances. His leadership approach is also emulated in a local school, which guarantees that every child receives an excellent education. He also recommended the establishment of an open university. It is known as the Indira Gandhi National Open University.
16.	Shri P.V. Narasimha Rao	25 September 1985 – 25 June 1988	2 years and 9 months	He was an Indian politician who served as the country's ninth Prime Minister. He is

S. No.	*Name of Education Ministers*	*Tenure*	*Duration*	*Past Works/About*
		25 December 1994 – 9 February 1995 17 January 1996 – 16 May 1996	3 months 5 months	known as the Father of Indian Economic Reforms. He oversaw a huge economic revolution and safeguarded India's national security when several domestic mishaps happened. Rao is primarily remembered for bringing down the Licence Raj and not much else. During the moment of transition in India, he handled the industries' portfolios. Natwar Singh, a former Foreign Minister said, 'Unlike Nehru, his knowledge of Sanskrit was profound. Nehru had a temper, PV a temperament. His roots were deep in the spiritual and religious soil of India. He did not need to "Discover India".'
17.	Shri P. Shiv Shankar	25 June 1988 – 2 December 1989	1 year and 6 months	P. Shiv Shankar helped people from all walks of life and strove to ameliorate the suffering of the poor at a period when poverty was still a big issue in India. He was a powerful Minister in Indira Gandhi and Rajiv Gandhi's cabinets, and he was one of India's most senior politicians. From 1994 to 1995, he was governor of Sikkim, and from 1995 to 1996, he was governor of Kerala.
18.	Shri V.P. Singh	2 December 1989 – 10 November 1990	1 year	During his time as Prime Minister, he put the Mandal Commission findings for India's backward castes into action. This sparked widespread opposition to the

S. No.	*Name of Education Ministers*	*Tenure*	*Duration*	*Past Works/About*
				measure. It resulted in the revocation of the 62nd Amendment, which established the Scheduled Castes and Scheduled Tribes Act. As Prime Minister, he looked over the Ministry of Education and strongly reflected on the pulling up of backward castes and minority groups. In the year 1992, he protested against the demolition of the Babri Masjid.
19.	Shri Rajmangal Pandey	21 November 1990 – 21 June 1991	8 months	He was an Indian politician who was a member of the Janata Dal. He formerly served in the ninth Lok Sabha, representing the Uttar Pradesh seat of Deoria. From 1990 to 1991, he was Minister of Human Resource Development in the Chandra Shekhar Cabinet.
20.	Shri Arjun Singh	23 June 1991 – 24 December 1994 22 May 2004 – 22 May 2009	3 years and 6 months 5 years	He won from the Satna Lok Sabha constituency in 1991. However, following Rajiv Gandhi's death, he resigned his assembly position and had hopes of becoming Prime Minister. P.V. Narasimha Rao was India's Prime Minister for approximately seven years, and following the demolition of the Babri Masjid in early 1992, he grew antagonistic towards Rao. Then, as Minister of Human Resource Development, Singh was appointed. He openly stated his displeasure with his

S. No.	*Name of Education Ministers*	*Tenure*	*Duration*	*Past Works/About*
				PM Rao, and resigned from his position.
21.	Shri Madhavrao Scindia	10 February 1995 – 17 January 1996	1 year	Scindia was the son of Jiwajirao Scindia, the last reigning Maharaja of Gwalior. Scindia inherited a privy purse, some rights, and the title 'Maharaja of Gwalior' after his father died in 1961. However, it only survived until 1971, when the 26th Amendment to the Indian Constitution dissolved all privileges to the erstwhile royals. Scindia is attributed to establishing the Indian Institute of Information Technology and Management (IIITM) in Gwalior as a reputable institution, which was renamed ABV-IIITM after Atal Bihari Vajpayee.
22.	Shri Atal Bihari Vajpayee	16 May 1996 – 1 June 1996	1 month	As Prime Minister, he witnessed two nuclear tests conducted by India on a regular basis, the first in 1974 and the second in 1998. He attempted to strengthen diplomatic relations with Pakistan by busing himself to Lahore to meet with Prime Minister Nawaz Sharif. Following the 1999 Kargil War, he attempted to repair relations with Pakistan by meeting with President Pervez Musharraf. He invited President Musharraf to India for a conference at Agra.

S. No.	*Name of Education Ministers*	*Tenure*	*Duration*	*Past Works/About*
23.	Shri S.R. Bommai	5 June 1996 – 19 March 1998	1 year and 9 months	He was given responsibility for the government's Industries portfolio. However, he quit after only a few months. Mr. Bommai is well-known for his commitment to ethics, and he served as the Chief Minister of Karnataka from 13th August 1988, until 1st October 1988. He was also active in the 1942 Quit India campaign, which helped establish the unified Karnataka state, which had previously been divided among Bombay Presidency, Mysore, Hyderabad, and Madras Presidency.
24.	Dr Murali Manohar Joshi	19 March 1998 – 22 May 2004	6 years and 2 months	Between 1991 to 1993, he served as President of the BJP and as a Member of Parliament for Kanpur. He used to be a physics professor at the University of Allahabad. He rose to prominence after becoming a significant figure in the BJP party. Later in his career, he served as a Human Resources Minister in the NDA administration. The Government of India bestowed the Padma Vibhushan, India's second highest civilian honour, to Joshi in 2017.
25.	Shri Kapil Sibal	29 May 2009 – 29 October 2012	3 years and 5 months	In 2005 and 2009, he had the opportunity to represent India at the World Economic Forum. He was present on both occasions in Davos, Switzerland. He headed the Indian team to the Annapolis

S. No.	*Name of Education Ministers*	*Tenure*	*Duration*	*Past Works/About*
				summit in November 2007 to garner worldwide support for the formation of a Palestinian State and the fulfilment of Israeli-Palestinian peace. In December 2007, he was a member of the Indian government to the United Nations Framework Convention on Climate Change (UNFCCC) in Bali.
26.	Shri M.M. Pallam Raju	30 October 2012 – 26 May 2014	1 years and 7 months	He is a member of the Indian National Congress and represents the constituency of Kakinada in Andhra Pradesh. He lost his mother early, but then decided to return to India and pursue a life in politics after his father had a stroke. He was not strongly encouraged by any family members, but he found success later on with the help of the right people. The general elections were held in 1989, and party members encouraged him to contest.
27.	Smt Smriti Irani	26 May 2014 – 5 July 2016	2 years and 2 months	She was a popular TV actress playing a role in the hit soap Kyunki Saas Bhi Kabhi Bahu Thi' She won the Amethi seat in the 2019 Indian general election, defeating Rahul Gandhi, the country's main opposition party leader and the President of the Indian National Congress. Irani was ushered in as a Cabinet Minister in May 2019 at the age of 43, making her the youngest minister in the 2019 Council of Ministers.

S. No.	*Name of Education Ministers*	*Tenure*	*Duration*	*Past Works/About*
				She has been part of the extensive exercise done for NEP in 2015, besides being instrumental in launching (GIAN), Swayam, Udaan Yojana, Pragati Scheme and NIRF rankings.
28.	Shri Prakash Javdekar	5 July 2016 – 30 May 2019	2 years and 10 months	Since his undergraduate days, Javdekar has been involved in Indian politics, and he was a member of the ABVP, the student organisation. He took part in anti-government protests during the Prime Minister's state of Emergency announcement. Javdekar served in the Bharatiya Janata Yuva Morcha as a National Secretary and later general secretary from 1984 until 1990. He joined the Bharatiya Janata Party as State Secretary and Campaign Chief in Maharashtra in 1989. He retained that role till 1991, when he was elected to the Maharashtra Assembly as a member of the Mohanpur Gafargaon seat. He went on to become the Executive President of the State Planning Board and later the Chairman of the Maharashtra government's IT task force.
29.	Shri Ramesh Pokhriyal 'Nishank'	30 May 2019 – 7 July 2021	2 year and 2 months	On 30 May, 2019, he was sworn in as Minister of Human Resource Development. India's Ministry of Education changed its name to Ministry of Education (India) in July 2020, and he resigned in July

S. No.	*Name of Education Ministers*	*Tenure*	*Duration*	*Past Works/About*
				2021 due to health issues. COVID-19 related issues landed him in the hospital for a month. He is now healthy and represents Haridwar in the 17th Lok Sabha. He won the Vatayan Lifetime Achievement Award while in office.
30.	Shri Dharmendra Pradhan	7 July 2021 – till now	Still running	He has served as Minister of Steel and Minister of Petroleum and Natural Gas. Pradhan is an Indian politician who serves in the Indian government as the Minister of Education and the Minister of Skill Development and Entrepreneurship. Pradhan, former professor of Computer Science, unveiled a number of programmes aimed at reskilling and upskilling India's workforce as well as closing the skill gap for Indian youth. During his tenure, the total number of Industrial Training Institutes (ITIs) grew by more than 40 per cent, and student enrolment grew by more than 28 per cent. He advocated new proposals for national education policy, such as eliminating NCVET and focusing on Industry 4.0 and skills development instead. He established Skill Saathi, a world-renowned flagship counselling programme. It is one of his finest efforts and has had a tremendous influence on the lives of countless individuals.

FIVE

The Resurgence

India, a Step Closer to Being a Knowledge Superpower

The highest education is that which does not merely give us information but makes our life in harmony with all existence.
– Rabindranath Tagore

The Birth of the New Education System

India is growing at a phenomenal rate in all fields, be it education, medicine, economy or other sectors. The current government of India is steering the country towards excellence, and is focussing a lot on education.

The population of India is huge, and therefore it holds great potential when it comes to human resources. The country needs an excellent and flexible education system as its backbone, and the current government seems to be working towards it. The plan of action seems to be to hold on to the values of the ancient educational system and alongside guide them on a path that enables them to compete with the rest of the world. Great initiatives by the government like Swachh Bharat Abhiyaan (Clean India Mission) and Digital India have proven the fact that India is moving towards betterment.

The new educational policies allow students to grow in a holistic and organic manner.

The NEP 2020

The National Education Policy 2020 clearly mentions: 'A high-quality higher education must enable personal achievement and enlightenment, constructive public engagement, and productive societal contribution. It must prepare students for more meaningful and fulfilling lives and jobs, as well as economic independence.'

The Union Cabinet of India approved the NEP 2020 on 29 July 2020, which defines the vision for India's new education system. The NEP 2020 supersedes the 34-year-old NPE of 1986 as the first education policy of the 21st century. A panel chaired by former Indian Space Research Organisation (ISRO) Chief Krishnaswamy Kasturirangan proposed the NEP in 2019. The government clarified that no one will be forced to study any particular language, and that the medium of teaching will not be changed from English to any regional language.

Numerous reforms to India's education policy are enacted by the NEP 2020. It aspires to raise expenditure on education from roughly 3 per cent to 6 per cent of the GDP. This policy intends to reduce student workloads and allow them to become more interdisciplinary and multilingual. Numerous new bodies and concepts, such as the National Education Commission, Academic Bank of Credit, National Research Foundation, Special Education Zones, and Gender Inclusion Fund, have been given legislative permission to be formed under NEP 2020.

The National Educational Policy of 2020 stresses on a skilled nation, and is determined to encounter problems faced by the education system with intergrity. These problems include:

- A highly fragmented higher education environment.
- The development of cognitive skills and learning outcomes receiving less attention.
- A strict division of subjects, with early specialisation and students flooding into limited fields of study.
- Limited access, especially in socio-economically challenged places where there are few Higher Education Institute Society (HEIS) that educate in local languages.
- Teacher and institutional autonomy are constrained.
- Academics and institutional leaders have insufficient procedures for merit-based career management and advancement.
- Most universities and colleges place less emphasis on research, and there is a dearth of competitive peer-reviewed research funding across fields, resulting in poor Higher Education Institutions' governance and leadership.
- Large affiliating institutions have an inadequate regulatory framework, resulting in low undergraduate education standards.

With the government and educational committee having acknowledged the problems in the educational system, the policy was put forward in order to welcome high-quality education in harmony with equality and inclusion. The vision of the policy includes the following:

- Working toward a higher education system with major, interdisciplinary universities and colleges in or near every district, as well as additional HEIs across India that provide local/Indian language mediums of instruction or programmes.
- Transitioning to a more heterogeneous undergraduate education.
- Faculty and institutional autonomy to become more important.
- Curriculum, pedagogy, assessment, and student assistance are all to be revamped in order to improve student experiences.
- Merit appointments and career development based on teaching, research, and service to reassert the integrity of academic and institutional leadership positions.
- Establishing a National Research Foundation to reward great peer-reviewed research and aggressively foster research in universities and colleges.
- HEIs are to be governed by highly competent independent boards with academic and administrative autonomy and subjected to mild but strict oversight by a single higher education authority.
- Higher education regulation that is 'light but tight' by a single regulator.
- Expanded access, equity, and inclusion through a variety of initiatives, including improved public education opportunities.
- Scholarships for disadvantaged and impoverished students from private/philanthropic institutions.
- Learners with disabilities should have access to online education, Open Distance Learning (ODL), and its infrastructure and learning resources.

Bringing Back the Essence of International Standards

Ancient universities like Takshashila and Nalanda attracted students from all over the world. They welcomed different cultures and languages, and diversified their subjects. The interactions between the teachers and the students left a mark on the history of Indian education. Following in the same footsteps, the NEP 2020 has brought major changes to the existing education system while maintaining the essence.

It is not only limited to providing higher education to students, but also focuses on uplifting the quality of education so that the Indian educational institutes are able to attract students from all over the world. The All-India Council for Technical Education, in its framework to categorise standalone institutions to enjoy considerable operational autonomy, states that, one of the criteria for being classified as Category I is that the institution be ranked among the top 500 of reputable world rankings, such as Quacquarelli Symonds (QS) or Times Higher Education (THE). With the help of government-funded policies, scholarships and schemes, efforts are being made to increase the global rankings of Indian institutes and push them to fetch greater testimonials. In the QS 2023 World University Ranking released on 8 June 2022, 27 universities were included in the top 1,000, with 9 of them featuring in the top 500, whereas the Times Higher Education (THE) World University Ranking 2023 included 37 universities in the top 1,000, with 5 of them in the top 500.

There is no doubt that India is the hub of good quality education as per international standards. The government is now working towards bringing all higher education institutions to a certain level to match standards internationally. The NEP 2020 is based on five pillars: Access, Equity, Quality, Affordability and Accountability. This educational reform is aimed at a paradigm transition by providing the students, teachers and educational institutions with the requisite competencies and capacities and creating, enabling and rejuvenating the education environment for a spectacular new India. The NEP guidelines will aid Indian higher education institutions in making a worldwide influence via systematic planning and delivery. It is critical that we keep up with developments and concerns in the worldwide higher education system in order to remain competitive for bright students. The following are the objectives put forward:

- Make India a desirable study location for international students.
- To help our professors and students develop international skills.
- To instil a global attitude in our students and mould them into global citizens who are proud to be Indian.
- Encourage strong collaboration between Indian and international higher education institutions.
- To increase the internationalisation metrics' worldwide ranking.

Renaming the Ministry

Initially, the education ministry was named the Ministry of Education, but things changed when the late Prime Minister Rajiv Gandhi led the government. During his time, the ministry was renamed the Ministry of Human Resource Department (MHRD). In 1984, his advisers suggested bringing all educational departments under one roof, and Rajiv Gandhi accepted it. The Ministry of Education was renamed the Ministry of Human Resource Development on 26 September 1985, and P.V. Narasimha Rao became the MHRD Minister. Ministers of state were appointed, and related departments such as Culture and Youth & Sports were integrated under the Ministry of HRD. Also, the Department of Women and Child Development was a department of the Union Ministry of Human Resources Development. The step was harshly criticised by many news reporters and people belonging to academic circles.

The name of the ministry was suggested to be altered again, according to a commission chaired by former ISRO chairman K. Kasturirangan. Later on, Ram Bahadur Rai, chairman of the Conference on Academic Leadership on Education for Resurgence's joint organising committee and head of the Indira Gandhi National Centre for the Arts, proposed yet another change. Many people wanted education to be a separate ministry and not to be part of an amalgamation. Thus, in the NEP 2020, to focus solely on education and under the direction of the current Prime Minister, the Ministry of Human Resources Department was changed to the Ministry of Education.

Journey to Becoming the Superpower of Knowledge

India is keen to bring back the glory of the past. Proper policies and the culture of modern infrastructure will put the education system on a forward path. Replicating other international educational institutions is not enough, and thus initiative has to be taken to empower the youth and bring flexibility to their courses. Since Independence, India's poverty line has come down, and so has the illiteracy rate. Only when households don't have to strain to get the bare minimum for existence can they afford to let their children pursue higher education. India is one of the fastest-growing economies in the world and its economy is set to become the superpower of knowledge. The country is catching up with many developed nations and has been able to provide a lot of opportunities for the people. With the rise in demand for high-quality content, India's education sector has seen an increase in international students as well as quality standards. With this increase in demand, Indian universities have also seen an increase in their revenues which has helped them expand their infrastructure and facilities. The Indian government is also focusing on making India a global powerhouse in artificial intelligence technologies with initiatives like 'Make in India' and 'Digital India'. This will also help it to be at par with other countries and states like China, the US, Japan, and others.

India has also been successfully diversifying its economy from agriculture to manufacturing to service sectors with increased investments in technology-intensive industries like IT/ITES, pharmaceuticals, biotechnology, aerospace engineering and defence manufacturing. India's economic growth is driven by a large number of factors, such as a young population, increasing urbanisation and industrialisation, and increasing government spending on education and health services.

Building the Brand of Higher Educational Institutions in India

Indian universities with international standards are becoming the norm. They not only provide high-quality education but also employ a large number of people. They also meet the demands of the country by delivering education in a variety of subjects and promoting the public interest through their programmes.

In today's India, universities are reaching out to international candidates and this is made possible by excellent communication which is boosted by the power of social media to spread the outreach of Indian educational brands. The following objectives were included in NEP 2020 in this regard:

- Creating a country-specific report based on academic and market research on prospective students' top goals.
- As a result, with the support of government and regulatory authorities, a country-specific plan to entice those potential students to study in India should be developed and implemented.
- Higher education institutions are encouraged to establish offshore campuses in order to broaden their reach and promote India as a study destination for overseas students. Eminent institutions have been granted permission to establish offshore campuses.
- Spreading information about India's education system, accreditation and ranking method.
- Scholarships are a critical component in attracting students to India. Higher education institutions should use their brand-building approach to incorporate information about current scholarships.

- Providing workshops, seminars, presentations and cultural activities at targeted institutions and target countries to raise awareness of educational possibilities in India and their institution.
- For brand-building exercises, collaborating with international alumni or alumni of Indian origin living abroad.
- Expanding the scope of Indian HEIs' online, open and remote learning courses through a systematic approach.
- Publicly announcing the educational system and institutions' best practices to the worldwide academic and research community.
- Promoting language courses, bridging courses and short-term non-degree specialised courses on Indian art and culture, yoga, Ayurveda and Buddhism, among other subjects.
- Such brand creation exercises make extensive use of the digital platform and virtual mode.

Connection with International Alumni

International alumni are like brand ambassadors and provide great connections with international educational institutes as well as the academic circle. An alumni can offer assistance and information, and help fund and organise outreach programmes. Indian students studying abroad are an integral element of India's higher education institutions' success. They not only reach out to other nations but also bring back fresh ideas that help progress global knowledge and place us on a worldwide platform. International students bring in a number of skills, global awareness, knowledge in the language of instruction, and more. They also act as managers for international students at their host institution. They are also experienced with the services like immigration processing and international student programming which boosts the confidence of other foreign students. The benefits to the host institution can be substantial and international students provide an economic boost to the country. India needs a greater number of alumni to be able to gain more economic and cultural benefits. In order to effectively connect alumni, higher education institutions in India must make alumni more visible. They also should create branding campaigns to raise awareness among students.

Significant Efforts by the Ministry of Education

Under the Ministry of Education (MoE), the Department of Higher Education focuses on providing plans and policies to build a strong foundation. Expansion of higher education institutes is done keeping qualitative education as the main aim. World-class colleges, universities and other educational establishments are given immense priority. The map of India is finely combed to set up well-structured and planned educational institutions. The vision of the Department of Higher Education is 'to realise India's human resource potential to its fullest in the Higher Education sector, with equity and inclusion.'

Establishing world-class colleges and universities is not enough and thus the Ministry of Education always roots for 'equality' and 'inclusion'. These two words are needed by students who do not have access to higher education. In the Preamble of the Indian Constitution, the word 'equality' holds a special place. Its significance is emphasised in all the departments and ministries of the Government of India.

An 18-year-old girl, living with her family in an extreme part of India, wants to pursue her higher education. Rough terrain surrounds her house and transportation is not like in urban places. In that instance, that girl needs programmes, schemes and scholarships to make her education affordable and reachable. The budding of new institutions is meant to facilitate higher education for more students. Apart from the expansion of buildings, distance learning courses have done wonders in reaching out to more Indian students. Since the COVID-19 pandemic, the online learning model has vividly found a strong stance worldwide. Thus, the online courses initiated by the MoE have helped many students continue their studies.

Schemes and Scholarships

The famous America Essayist, Ralph Waldo Emerson said, 'Scholarship is to be created not by compulsion, but by awakening a pure interest in knowledge'. This awakening and strengthening of the youth of the country were brought about by the Ministry of Education through schemes and scholarships. The following is the list of university and higher education schemes:

- Rashtriya Uchchatar Shiksha Abhiyan (RUSA)
- National Initiative for Design Innovation
- National Research Professorship
- Establishment of New Central Universities
- Indira Gandhi National Tribal University
- Establishment of 14 world-class central universities

- Setting up of 374 degree colleges in educationally backward districts
- Scheme for incentivising state governments for the expansion of higher education institutions
- Construction of girls' hostels
- Supporting uncovered state universities and colleges
- Strengthening science-based higher education and research in universities
- Inter Universities Research Institute for Policy and Evaluation
- Additional assistance to about 160 already covered universities and 5,500 colleges
- Schemes implemented through statutory and autonomous organisations

For technical education, the following schemes are implemented:

- Sub-Mission on Polytechnics under the Coordinated Action for Skill Development
- National Scheme of Apprenticeship Training
- Support For Distance Education & Web-Based Learning (NPTEL)
- Indian National Digital Library in Engineering, Science & Technology (INDEST-AICTE) Consortium
- Technology Development Mission
- Direct admission of students abroad
- Setting up 20 new IIITs
- Establishment of centres of excellence in frontier areas of science and technology
- IMPRINT (Impacting Research in Technology)
- Ucchatar Avishkar Yojana

The MoE has a huge budget for schemes and scholarships. For example, the RUSA scheme has an expenditure of Rs 12,929.16 crore which is divided among the central government and the state governments as Rs 8,120.97 crore and Rs 4,808.19 crore respectively. According to the National Initiative for Design Innovation scheme, each Design Innovative Centre is getting 10 crore. Under the technical scheme of Sub-Mission on Polytechnics under the Coordinated Action for Skill Development, 500 polytechnics will get 2 crore each. The establishment of 14 world-class central universities scheme saw an 18.5 per cent increase in funds and currently, the MoE allocated Rs 1,04,277 crore for the purpose. Allocation in Union Budget 2021–22 strongly saved a huge portion for the Department of Higher Education. 41 per cent of all the ministries' total fund was given to the Department of Higher Education and it was Rs 38,351 crore.

Since 2014, the Ministry of Education introduced schemes for the betterment of technical learning and skill development. A lot of priority is given to uplifting the youth in developing their technical education and skills. In addition, science and research form the fundamentals of new inventions and discoveries. Thus, great initiatives have been taken to facilitate the candidates with good infrastructure, updated equipment and advanced guidance. The MoE has been resourceful in establishing excellent centres in the scientific and technological arenas. Technology driving the masses is a great source of ease for our modern world. India has to be at par with other advanced scientific research and technological developments.

Academic Bank of Credits, also known as ABC, is a vital part of the National Education Policy of 2020. It guarantees that a student's credits from one institution are transferred to another with his or her approval. The easy transfer of credits helps students go from one institution to the next. Credits are automatically awarded to students who complete any course and pass the tests. Institutions must fill out the necessary information and submit deposits to the individuals' Academic Credit Bank accounts using the digital portal. The ABC does the following:

- Increases the choice of courses and disciplines available to students.
- Allows students to drop out at any time throughout the year and, if qualified, exchange their credits for a certificate or diploma.
- They might use the credits to return to the same or another institute and finish their study.
- Institutes cannot force students to attend classes against their choice in order to make money.

Scholarships add wings for a merited student to fly. There are a variety of scholarships available to students. Some scholarships are based on merit, while others are based on financial need. Merit-based scholarships are awarded to students who have achieved academic excellence or demonstrated exceptional talent in a specific area. Financial need-based scholarships are awarded to students who come from low-income families or who have demonstrated financial need. Some of the national scholarships available to students are:

- Special Scholarship Scheme for Jammu & Kashmir.

- Central Sector Scheme of Scholarships for college and university students.
- Scheme for Scholarship to students from non-Hindi speaking states for post Matric studies in Hindi.

Economy and Education

The economy of India is dependent on high-quality education. India is now the world's second-most populous country with over 1.38 billion people, and it is projected to be the world's most populous country by 2027. In order to sustain the economic growth and development in the country, it is very important to have a large population that is educated and skilled. According to a recent study by the World Bank, India's GDP could grow by an additional 1.5 per cent to 2 per cent every year over the next two decades if the country manages to increase its average level of education. The Indian economy is one of the fastest-growing economies in the world. The government has been making efforts to improve the quality of education in India. The Right to Education Act has been like an umbrella to ensure that all children in India receive free and compulsory education.

At the end of the day, people opt for good value for money and to attract foreign investments in the country, the higher education of the youth plays an immense part. India is known to be a land of talents. It has given the world some great minds to run international companies like Sundar Pichai (chief executive officer of Alphabet. Inc and Google), Indra Nooyi (chief executive officer of PepsiCo), Leena Nair (chief executive officer of Chanel), Shantanu Narayen (chief executive officer of Adobe Systems) and many more. There are many talented and genius students from India who immigrate to more developed countries to pursue their higher education, commit to a job or start a business. The current government is setting up a framework to provide world-class facilities to students. In the national building process, great minds are needed in all fields. Thus, the Indian government is working towards keeping talent within the country.

Digital India and Digital Education

The Government of India has embarked on an ambitious mission to connect all citizens of India with the digital world. This initiative is known as 'Digital India'. The goal of Digital India is to provide all citizens of India with access to the internet so that they can participate in the digital economy. The government has undertaken a number of initiatives to achieve this goal. These initiatives include the development of a nationwide broadband network, the promotion of digital literacy, and the provision of financial incentives to businesses that adopt digital technologies. The government has also established a number of Centres of Excellence to promote the adoption of digital technologies.

India has made giant strides in the digital domain in the past few years. The Digital India programme, which was launched by Prime Minister Narendra Modi in 2015, has been pivotal in this transformation. Under the Digital India initiative, the government has been working towards connecting rural areas with high-speed internet, providing digital literacy training to citizens, and making government services available online. Private players have also been coming up with innovative digital solutions to cater to the needs of Indian consumers. The initiative has three core components:

- Providing broadband connectivity to all citizens.
- Creating digital infrastructure and platforms for delivering government services.
- Using digital technologies to make government processes more efficient.

The impact of the Digital India initiative has been significant. It has led to an increase in internet penetration, the number of people using digital services, and the number of start-ups. The initiative has also helped to create jobs, boost economic growth, and improve social inclusion.

Digital education pulls in a lot of weight in the future growth of India. It is gradually gaining a foothold in the country. With the increasing penetration of the internet and smartphones, more and more people are getting connected to the digital world. This is opening up new avenues for learning and education. There are various platforms available for digital education in India. These include online courses, Massive Open Online Courses (MOOCs), and E-learning platforms. Many top universities in India have started offering online courses. This provides students with an opportunity to learn from some of the best professors in the country without having to leave their homes. The Indian government is also making efforts to promote digital education.

It is seen as the future of education, and for good reason. There are a number of advantages to digital education that are making it a popular choice among students and parents alike.

Some of the advantages of digital education include:

- **Accessibility:** Digital education can be accessed from anywhere in the world, at any time. This makes it a very convenient option for students who want to continue their education while working or travelling. Students do not have to worry about missing classes. Recorded online courses help students to learn according to their preferences.
- **Affordability:** Digital education is often more affordable than traditional education methods. This is because all educational elements are in digital mode. Information and knowledge are shown on the electronic display instead of getting printed on paper. That saves a lot of money and supports sustainability!

Strengthening Vocational Trainings and Skill Developments Across Ages

Skill-based vocational training and education have been an integral part of the Indian education system for a very long time now. However, the quality and efficacy of these programmes have been a matter of concern for quite some time. There is an urgent need to strengthen these programmes and make them more relevant to the needs of the industry and the students. The government has taken some steps in this direction, but a lot more needs to be done which the government is meaning to do. The private sector needs to come forward and collaborate with the government to improve the quality and relevance of vocational training and education in India.

There are many works that have been carried on for generations after generations. To break free and make education malleable among the mass, vocational training in different subjects have been a great foundation for people to break free from the strains of lineage work. There is a lot of art and machinery which have taken a hefty fall. Thus to be at pace with the modern world, the traditional ways do need a little tweaking. While the outcome can remain the same, the process of making the product should match the demands of the marketplace.

In recent years, the collaboration between SWAYAM and National Programme on Technology Enhanced Learning (NPTEL) has benefitted many university students as well as people of all ages. The programme

SWAYAM was formed by the Government of India and the objective was 'to take the best teaching learning resources to all, including the most disadvantaged'. It aims to close the digital barrier for students who are left behind by the digital revolution and are unable to participate fully in the economy of knowledge. Under the SWAYAM roof, nine national coordinators that have been appointed:

- All India Council for Technical Education (AICTE) for self-paced and international courses.
- National Programme on Technology Enhanced Learning (NPTEL) for engineering.
- University Grants Commission (UGC) for non-technical post-graduation education.
- Consortium for Educational Communication (CEC) for undergraduate education.
- National Council of Educational Research and Training (NCERT) for school education.
- Institute of Open Schooling (IOS) for school education.
- Indira Gandhi National Open University (IGNOU) for out-of-school students.
- Indian Institute of Management, Bangalore (IIMB) for management studies.
- National Institute of Technical Teachers Training and Research (NITTTR) for teacher training programmes.

Bringing Back the Lost Lustre: A Multi-disciplinary Approach

Since the Narendra Modi government took charge, there have been motives to bring back the lost essence of ancient India. The cultures that got buried in the subconsciousness of Indian people have once again started coming to the fore. India is proud to be a secular country that gives space and respect to different religions and belief systems. Alongside exist spiritual practices like yoga, aided by Ayurveda and educational excellence, making India truly a global power.

Rejuvenation of Nalanda University

Emulating the long-lost ancient university of Nalanda, a new Nalanda University was established after an Act by the Parliament in 2010. The architectural design of the rejuvenated university was such that it is at par with other international universities. The primary notion behind the building of the university included 'advancing the concept of an Asian community and rediscovering old relationships,' and 'acting as a bridge for students in different parts of Southeast Asia.'

During the second East Asia Summit, the idea to rebuild Nalanda University was validated by 16 member countries in 2007. Following such huge support, at the fourth East Asia summit in 2009, the ASEAN members China, Australia, Singapore, Korea and Japan assured further support. The university is envisioned as a nationally significant and excellent worldwide institution. On 1 September 2014, the resurrected Nalanda University started its very first academic session with only 15 students in the School of Ecology and Environmental Studies and the School of Historical Studies. A nearby hotel under the Bihar State Tourism Development Corporation facilitated the students with hostel accommodation. 80 per cent of the campus developments had been completed by 2021, and further work is going on.

Spreading the Wellness of Yoga

When was the first time you heard the word yoga? Did you ever wonder where this word came from? The word 'yoga' means addition or union. It stands for the union of physical, mental and spiritual dimensions of life. The ancient texts of the Vedas first coined the term yoga. It was mentioned in the *Rigveda* which thorough practices have been well described to stay balanced, peaceful and well. To practise yoga is to go beyond the physical realms of life and seek spiritual connections of the body with the universe.

In recent years, the trend of going to yoga classes in Western countries has gained a lot of momentum. People living in other parts of the world welcomed the goodness of yoga like any other household chore. The yoga that is cultivated in the western world is known as *Hatha Yoga* (physical fitness that is posture-based). Welcoming the *asanas* (body posture) into their lives, many people felt that the contents of ancient Indian scriptures were effectively working with the modern lives of people. There are many things that have changed over decades—lifestyles, technicalities of executing work, geography and more. As humans are adapting to the new changes and technological advancements, ancient yoga has provided a deep level of comfort, mindfulness and satisfaction.

To nurture not just physical betterment but also the mental and spiritual aspects of yoga, Prime Minister Narendra Modi put forward the suggestion in his UN speech on 27 September 2014, to observe 'Yoga Day' as an occasion. Following that in 2015, in favour of global health and peace, International Yoga Day was announced and is celebrated annually on 21 June. Across the world, people take the initiative to inculcate this practice into their daily life to foster spiritual growth.

Sanskrit: Ancient Language, New Universities

Sanskrit, the classical language of India, is one of the oldest and most complex languages in the world. It is a member of the Indo-European family of languages and is related to both Hindi and Persian. Sanskrit is an interesting language because it has both a modern and an ancient form. The modern form is used for writing and communication, while the ancient form is used for religious ceremonies and spiritual purposes. Sanskrit is also one of the few living Indo-European languages that still have a significant number of speakers. It is the ancient Indian language which is still in use today. It is the language of Hindu religious texts and classical Indian music and dance. It is also one of the 22 official languages of India. It is a difficult language to learn, but it is very rich in vocabulary. It has a complex grammatical structure and is phonetically precise. Sanskrit is the ancestor of all the modern Indian languages.

Sanskrit universities were set up primarily to promote the Sanskrit language and culture, but over the years they have evolved into comprehensive institutions of learning. The Sanskrit universities are known for their high level of scholarship. They offer a wide range of courses in the Sanskrit language and literature. The students at these universities are highly motivated, and many of them go on to become leading scholars and professionals. The Sanskrit universities also serve as a repository of India's cultural heritage. They promote the study and appreciation of traditional Indian arts and sciences.

As envisaged in the new National Education Policy (NEP), the government has given importance to all Indian languages, including Sanskrit.

Make in India: Supporting India's Journey Towards Becoming a Knowledge Superpower

India has made significant strides in the past few years to become a self-reliant economy. The country has made a concerted effort to boost its manufacturing sector, with the aim of reducing its dependence on imports. The 'Make in India' campaign was launched in September 2014, with the goal of growing India into a global manufacturing hub. The campaign has been successful in attracting foreign investors and boosting the country's manufacturing sector. The Make in India push is part of the Modi government's bigger aim to make India a worldwide leader in a variety of fields. India has made impressive progress in areas such as renewable energy and resources. The government has also been working on it along with other initiatives such as 'Digital India' and 'Skill India' to improve the quality of life of citizens and to make the country more technologically advanced. These initiatives have started to show results, and foreign investors are now starting to invest in India.

India has been a hub of manufacturing and exporting for a long time. With the advent of the Make in India campaign, the country has seen a significant surge in exports, both in terms of value and volume. There are some sectors that have seen the highest growth in exports due to the Make in India campaign: automobiles, electrical machinery, textiles, leather goods, gems and jewellery. The campaign, which was launched in September 2014, encourages companies to manufacture products in India, with the goal of increasing the country's share of global manufacturing from 17 to 25 per cent. The campaign has been successful in attracting a number of foreign investors. In the past year, investments from Japan, the US and South Korea alone have totalled $22 billion. This has helped to create jobs and increase the country's growth rate.

The 21st century is the century of knowledge. The world has become a global village and countries are striving to be the best in terms of education, technology and economy. India has always been a powerhouse in the field of education. But under the current government, the right executions are taking place. With an ever-increasing population of young people, India is well on its way to becoming the world's next knowledge superpower. The rise of digital India is a major contributing factor to this. With initiatives such as Digital India and Make in India, the country is rapidly moving towards a cashless, paperless and plastic economy. In addition, India has a large English-speaking population, which makes it an attractive destination for multinational companies looking to outsource their knowledge-based work. India also has a strong education system, with over 1,300 universities and 43,000 colleges. The country is home to some of the best engineering and management schools in the world.

Conclusion

India has always valued knowledge and its people have become torchbearers in many fields.

Whether it is digging up the mysteries, dusting off doubts or discovering the light of knowledge, it has formed a strong foundation of wisdom since ancient times. The rich cultural heritage of India has added to that knowledge and wisdom. Teachers have conveyed knowledge to their students in various ways. We have come a long way from only boys receiving formal education to girls topping every field. After the establishment of great universities like Nalanda, all students regardless of religion, caste, sex or creed were welcomed into the educational field. Initially, all lessons were through oral teachings. Ancient India became the first land to foster international universities and they were mostly funded by the kings and patrons of different regions. Knowledge was the weapon that could outwit a king's army.

The gates of ancient Indian universities were opened to international students. India was a knowledge superpower and through word of mouth, the depth of its education spread across the globe. Teachings were conducted in traditional languages, and Sanskrit became a global language. Many foreign students learnt different subjects like medicine, astrology and mathematics in Sanskrit. India offered a hospitable environment and brilliant students were attracted to its universities.

While Hinduism was the predominant culture of India, people of the land also immersed themselves in the teachings of Buddhism. Both religions had distinctive features and at the same time, they also had common ways of life and teachings. Along these cultures came people from neighbouring countries, influencing the formation of new lifestyles. Traders from China, Afghanistan and Sri Lanka would cross seas and mountains to sell their products and make profits. They brought along their cultures with them, and India became a diverse land.

With the emergence of Islamic rule in India, the addition of new language and literature influenced the teachings. Among the many influences, the excellent administration of the Mughal empire impacted the education system the most. The early Mughal rulers, especially Akbar, were liberal and therefore encouraged an atmosphere that was inclusive of all religions. Equal importance was given to Hindus, Buddhists and Muslims and their respective cultures and languages. However, corruption, imbalance and divisions on the basis of religion could not be kept at bay. Naturally, invasions and wars took place that caused division among kings and their subjects and altered the education system.

The rich subcontinent invited not only traders from neighbouring countries but also from faraway lands, across the seas. Portuguese travellers discovered India and were amazed by the spices and other rich products. They started trading and coastal areas became hubs for the spice trade. For over 450 years, Goa was a prime spot for the Portuguese empire and it was the beginning of colonisation in India. The fragrance of spices reached European countries and the East India Company unloaded its ships at the port of Calcutta. In the beginning, the intention of the East India Company was simply to trade. Just like the Portuguese, they traded in Indian spices, cotton, silk, saltpetre, indigo, tea opium and a few more products. Soon, European competitors started to emerge.

This competition pushed the East India Company to conquer regions in India. The company gathered military power and fought the battles of Plassey in 1757 and Buxar in 1764 on behalf of the British Crown. East India Company gained the *Diwani* (the right to handle the administration and collect revenue of a region) of Bengal. In a nutshell, the East India Company ruled Bengal on behalf of the British Crown. In the initial years, the British did not want Indians to learn the English language. They believed that Indians might pose challenges to the company's rule. But while running the administration of the country, the British people accepted the need for labour. Thus, was passed the English Education Act of 1835 which opened the doors for Indians to learn the English language and its literature. Soon, the company started to recruit Indian people who were well-versed in English into the administration of the British Raj.

What no one saw coming was the Indian Rebellion of 1857. Both Hindus and Muslims rose against the East India Company which led to much damage for the British. To take control and sublimate the situation, the Government of India Act 1858 was introduced. It brought India under the direct control of the British Raj.

From each province having its own king to being under a foreign ruler was a drastic change. As the Imperial Rule gave importance to English education, Indians started to learn the language. Schools, colleges and universities adopted the new curriculum and new establishments of education came about to transform Indians. Every province of India had to follow the English education system and have a university. English was given priority as a first language. Racism persisted as the British looked down on Indians. Cheap labour was readily available in India and the Indian supplies were great to trade in the European markets. Indians were forced to adapt to the new education system and it took away their opportunity to pursue higher education in the original languages of India.

India being divided into provinces meant that the *Zamindari* way of collecting revenues prevailed, which benefited the British. They collected taxes from poor farmers who worked on their land, irrespective of factors like whether the harvest was good or not, and whether the weather was conducive to farming or not. In 1770, after the East India Company was granted the Diwani of Bengal, the first Bengal Famine took between seven to ten million lives. The British showed no sympathy for the lives that were being lost. At the same time, they did not bother to reduce the taxes. It is documented that the price of rice reached three times its regular value and it left people starving.

Women crossed the threshold of their homes to pursue higher education at provincial institutions. With this, attitudes that separated women from the rest of the world began to fade. Women also spoke about their political rights, which Indian authorities enthusiastically backed. Political tensions in India developed from 1857 to 1902 as a result of the awakening and fervour for independence. Private institutions sprung up and spread in the years after 1921. It was a period when India yearned to have control of its own affairs. The educational systems of the British Indian government could not keep up with the expansion of private colleges and institutes. The Calcutta University Commission emphasised the need for coordinating university activities. The Lytton Committee in England had a similar opinion on the suggestions. Authorities wanted Indian undergraduates to have coordinated courses, and the Empire's universities to have higher education curriculum connections.

From the first to the third era of the British administration, the government's interest in Indian education waned. Prior to 1859, the central government controlled much of the income, and regional governments had little input in how the school system was changed. The bond between the Indian government and Indian education hit rock bottom between 1921 and 1937. During its early years of rule, the East India Company did not view the development of education as its responsibility or concern. Before any sort of education system was created for the Indian people, the British had been in India for a long time. The British government and society did not treat Indians well. In addition, the British government enacted rules that made it difficult for Indians to get employment and education. The British were able to establish their control and policies in India throughout the British–India period. Divide and conquer was the fundamental philosophy that guided the British Indian policy.

The torture, ill-treatment, partiality, racism and causing division among people became apparent to Indians. It was the Bengal province that first rose against British Rule and it did cause significant shock waves. India realised that uniting was the only way out. The British Education system failed the students badly.

There was an upsurge in revolts against the cruel British Rule. Provinces united to protest and the leadership of Mahatma Gandhi brought non-violence into the mainstream protest. The Non-Cooperation Movement, Civil Disobedience Movement, Dandi March, Satyagrah Andolan and many other forms of non-violent protests were initiated

Storms and tears ignited the youth of the country. Streets, roads and government buildings saw the fury of the people for India was determined to not bow down to the British Crown anymore. The external push from Azad Hind Fauj and the internal push from the rest of India led the British people to give back the baton of rule to the people of India. However, while leaving, the Crown divided the land and formed two separate nations—India and Pakistan.

Pakistan chose to become an Islamic state while India was determined to dip its feet into secularism. India had Hindu people as the majority but also cherished its diversity. As the partition took place in 1947, millions of people crossed the borders from both sides. Around 10 to 20 million people were displaced from their homes to find refuge in the newly formed nations. The displacement also took innocent lives of 200,000 to two million. The just-formed governments failed to bring order to the migration of such a huge mass. Many students had to face disruption in studies and work. To many students, education became a distant dream due to high levels of poverty.

When India got its independence, the literacy rate was only 12 per cent. It was a great concern for India and the high levels of poverty made it worse. The then government thought of replicating world-class Western universities in India. With external support, engineering, medical and other educational institutes were established. The drag-and-drop method of the education system at that time gave high-quality education only for limited streams and subjects. There was hardly any initiative to develop the skills of the youth and encourage people to pursue higher education. India was the second-most populous country and thus human resource was abundant. But still, there was no proper programme, scheme or scholarship to support the many brilliant minds. The education system was more exclusive than inclusive. Its selectiveness stepped down on the aspirations of many youths as it lacked flexibility.

When most of the people in the country dwelled in poverty, then filling up their stomachs was more important than rooting for higher education. There are many reasons why poverty affected higher education in India. Firstly, poor families were less likely to be able to afford the fees for private colleges, which were often the only ones with good facilities and quality teaching staff. It meant that their children were less likely to get a good education. Secondly, poverty often meant that people had to work long hours just to survive, which left little time for study. Finally, poverty led to poor health, which made it difficult to concentrate on learning. It is estimated that only a small fraction of the population had access to quality higher education. This was a major problem for the country, as it limited the potential of its people and prevented India from becoming a world leader in education.

The education system in India was inflexible and did not allow for skill development before the Modi government came into power. The Modi government has made significant changes to the education policy, making it more flexible and allowing for skill development. As a result, more students are now able to access quality education and develop the skills they need to succeed in the workforce.

The government under Prime Minister Narendra Modi introduced the National Education Policy 2020 (NEP 2020). It was released by the government on 29 July 2020. It aims to provide universal access to quality education for all by 2030. The policy also aims to improve the learning outcomes of all students and make India a global education hub. Some of the key reforms proposed in the policy are: the establishment of a National Higher Education Regulatory Authority, the setting up of a National Accreditation Framework, the establishment of a National Research Foundation, promoting the internationalisation of education, creating of a fund for the development of higher education, implementation of a credit-based system, setting up of a National Academic Depository and encouraging online and distance learning. The policy is a welcome step in the right direction and will go a long way in improving the quality of higher education in India. There are some more initiatives by the current government that are trying to improve the situation. The government has started to invest more in public universities and there are also some private organisations that are providing scholarships to bright students from poor families.

There is no doubt that India is becoming a knowledge superpower. With the expansion of world-class institutions, a booming economy and a population of young, highly-educated people, India is well on its way to becoming a leading global hub for knowledge and innovation. There are many reasons for this. Firstly, India is expanding its world-class institutions, such as the Indian Institutes of Technology (IITs), which are producing some of the world's top engineers and scientists. Secondly, India's economy is booming, making it an attractive destination for foreign investment and talent. And finally, India has a large population of young, highly-educated people who are eager to contribute to the country's development. All of these factors are coming together to create a perfect storm of knowledge and innovation in India. With the right policies and investments, India has the potential to become a world leader in knowledge and innovation.

The 'Make in India' campaign is a flagship initiative of the Government of India that was launched in September 2014. The primary objective of the campaign is to boost the manufacturing sector in India and make it a global leader. Quality education is the backbone of any nation's development and the Make in India campaign recognises this fact. The Make in India initiative has been successful in attracting foreign investment and creating jobs. To truly make India a manufacturing powerhouse, the government focused on improving the quality of education. This is because quality education is the key to unlocking the potential of the workforce. Investing in quality education will not only boost the Make in India campaign, but will also lay the foundations for a prosperous future for India. It is therefore crucial that the Government of India continues to invest in education so that we can realise our dream of making India a manufacturing powerhouse too.

References

Chapter 1: Learning Centres of Ancient India – Imparting Holistic Knowledge

Anant Sadashiv Altekar. (2009). *Education in ancient India*. Isha Books.

Barua, J. (2016). *Ancient BUDDHIST UNIVERSITIES in Indian Sub-Continent*. Fulton Books, Inc.

Britannica, T. Editors of Encyclopaedia (2018, October 26). Nalanda. Encyclopedia Britannica. https://www.britannica.com/topic/Nalanda

Chaube, S. P. (1988). *History and Problems of Indian Education: Discussing Salient Features from Ancient to Modern Times and Highlighting the Basic Issues and Trends for To-day and Tomorrow*. Vinod Pustak Mandir.

Clarification. (2011, September 19). *The Hindu*. https://www.thehindu.com/features/kids/clarification/article2467247.ece#:

Examrace. (2020, June 18). *Ancient Universities: Nalanda, Takshila, Vikramshila, Valabhi| Aryabhatt, Nagarjuna, Kautilya | NET*. Www.youtube.com. https://www.youtube.com/watch?v=VqEACkzNs3I

FactStar. (2021, April 5). *Why did Khilji destroy Nalanda University? | FactStar*. Www.youtube.com. https://www.youtube.com/watch?v=bE4-WQowVZg

Glavin, C. (2019, March 12). *History of Higher Education in India | K12 Academics*. Www.k12academics.com. https://www.k12academics.com/Higher%20Education%20Worldwide/Higher%20Education%20in%20India/history-higher-education-india#:~:text=The%20first%20institution%20of%20higher

Haridas, A. (2018). *Kanthalloor Sala: The 1000-year-old university in Trivandrum you may not have heard of*. Edex Live. https://www.edexlive.com/beinspired/2018/apr/18/kanthalloor-sala-the-1000-year-old-university-in-trivandrum-you-may-not-have-heard-of-2515.html

Harshananda. (2007). *An introduction to Hindu culture*. Advaita Ashrama, Publication Dept.

After Nalanda, another university remains found in Bihar. (2014, January 15). Www.thehindubusinessline.com. https://www.thehindubusinessline.com/news/education/After-Nalanda-another-university-remains-found-in-Bihar/article20712084.ece

Ancient institutions of learning in the Indian subcontinent. (2022). Wikipedia. https://en.wikipedia.org/wiki/Ancient_institutions_of_learning_in_the_Indian_subcontinent

Bakhtiyar Khalji - Banglapedia. (2021). Banglapedia.org. https://en.banglapedia.org/index.php/Bakhtiyar_Khalji

Government of India, All India Council for Technical Education. (2022). Www.aicte-India.org. https://www.aicte-india.org

History and Revival – Nalanda University. (2019). Nalanda University. https://nalandauniv.edu.in/about-nalanda/history-and-revival/

Maitraka dynasty. (2022, October 21). Wikipedia. https://en.wikipedia.org/wiki/Maitraka_dynasty

Immortal Bharat. (2019, February 10). *Part 1 – Education in Ancient India*. Www.youtube.com. https://www.youtube.com/watch?v=M79C3dSB90A

Immortal Bharat. (2021, May 3). *Part 2 – Destruction of Indian Education System by Islamic Invaders*. Www.youtube.com. https://www.youtube.com/watch?v=I5orKo5Mie0

Nalanda. (2020, February 16). Wikipedia. https://en.wikipedia.org/wiki/Nalanda

Inamdar, M. (2021a, March 16). *India's 5 Glorious Ancient Universities, which were destroyed by invasion*. Trunicle. https://trunicle.com/indias-5-glorious-ancient-universities-which-were-destroyed-by-invasion/

Inamdar, M. (2021b, March 16). *India's 5 Glorious Ancient Universities, which were destroyed by invasion*. Trunicle. https://trunicle.com/indias-5-glorious-ancient-universities-which-were-destroyed-by-invasion/

Soul of India: Timeline | Wide Angle | PBS. (2002, September 19). Wide Angle. https://www.pbs.org/wnet/wideangle/uncategorized/soul-of-india-timeline/2944/

Tajik Arabs – descendants of immigrants who at one time actively spread Islam in the region. (2019, September 5). CABAR.asia. https://cabar.asia/en/?p=23843#:~:text=05.09.2019-

Taxila. (2020). Wikipedia. https://en.wikipedia.org/wiki/Taxila

Tourism boost to historic Telhara. (2011). Www.telegraphindia.com. https://www.telegraphindia.com/bihar/tourism-boost-to-historic-telhara/cid/377651

Kosambi, D. D. (2016). *An introduction to the study of Indian history*. Sage.

Puri, B. Nath (2022, September 27). Taxila. Encyclopedia Britannica. https://www.britannica.com/place/Taxila

Rawat, P. L. (1981). *History of Indian education*. Agra Ram Prasad.

Sahana Singh. (2017). *The educational heritage of Ancient India : how an ecosystem of learning was laid to waste*. Chennai Notion Press, Inc.

Shastri, H. (1947). THE FALL OF THE VALABHI KINGDOM. *Proceedings of the Indian History Congress, 10*, 238–241. http://www.jstor.org/stable/44137138

StudyIQ IAS. (2021, November 10). *Why Bakhtiyar Khilji destroy ancient Nalanda University? Facts about Nalanda Mahavihara | 67th BPSC*. Www.youtube.com. https://www.youtube.com/watch?v=VVPEMygA9B8

Chapter 2: The Lost Lustre – Indian Education During British Era

Arun Banerii. (1984). British Rule and the Indian Economy: Agenda for Fresh Searches. *Economic and Political Weekly, 19*(31/33), 1273–1284. http://www.jstor.org/stable/4373481

Beno, Michal. (2019). The implications of the Industrial Revolutions for Higher Education.

Bhaskar, A. (2020, November 7). *Macaulay's View of Western Superiority Still Holds Back the Indian Education System*. The Wire. https://thewire.in/education/lord-macaulay-superior-view-western-hold-back-indian-education-system

Britannica, T. Editors of Encyclopaedia (2020, September 25). Industrial Revolution Causes and Effects. Encyclopedia Britannica. https://www.britannica.com/summary/Industrial-Revolution-Causes-and-Effects

Britannica, T. Editors of Encyclopaedia (2022, August 12). noncooperation movement. Encyclopedia Britannica. https://www.britannica.com/event/noncooperation-movement

Chand, B. (2017). *Advance Philosophy of Education*. Notion Press.

Chandra, B., Mukherjee, M., Mukherjee, A., Panikkar, K. N., & Mahajan, S. (2016). India's Struggle for Independence. In *Google Books*. Penguin UK.

Experts, D. (2021). *Indian History, Culture & Panorama Quick Revision Material for UPSC & State PSC General Studies Exams*. Disha Publications.

Hossain, A. (2022). *Colonial Globalization and its Effects on South Asia*. Taylor & Francis.

Abul Kalam Azad. (2019, September 26). Wikipedia; Wikimedia Foundation. https://en.wikipedia.org/wiki/Abul_Kalam_Azad

B. R. Ambedkar. (2019, February 13). Wikipedia; Wikimedia Foundation. https://en.wikipedia.org/wiki/B._R._Ambedkar

English Education Act 1835. (2019, December 20). Wikipedia; Wikimedia Foundation. https://en.wikipedia.org/wiki/English_Education_Act_1835

History of education in the Indian subcontinent. (2019, November 3). Wikipedia; Wikimedia Foundation. https://en.wikipedia.org/wiki/History_of_education_in_the_Indian_subcontinent

Non-cooperation movement. (2019, September 10). Wikipedia; Wikimedia Foundation. https://en.wikipedia.org/wiki/Non-Cooperation_Movement

Public health system in India. (2020, March 30). Wikipedia. https://en.wikipedia.org/wiki/Public_health_system_in_India

Jain, M. A. (2018, September 30). Racism and stereotypes in colonial India's "Instagram." *BBC News*. https://www.bbc.com/news/world-asia-india-45506092

Kochhar, S. K. (1995). *Pivotal Issues in Indian Education*. Sterling Publishers Pvt. Ltd.

Kumar, D. M., & Rekha, D. N. (2020). *Historical And Political Economy Of Education In India*. Sankalp Publication.

Kundu, A., & Mohanan, P. C. (2009). *Employment and inequality outcomes in India.* Jawaharlal Nehru University/Indian Statistical Service.

Mahmood, S. (1895). A History of English Education in India: Its Rise, Development, Progress, Present Condition and Prospects, Being a Narrative of the Various Phases of Educational Policy and Measures Adopted Under the British Rule from Its Beginning to the Present Period, (1781 to 1893)... In *Google Books.* M.A.O. College.

Maina Chawla Singh (2000) Philanthropy, Voluntarism, and Women's Education in Colonial India: A Study of the Bethune School, Calcutta, Asian Journal of Women's Studies, 6:3, 65-92, DOI: 10.1080/12259276.2000.11665886

Manas Chutia, Growth and Development of Education in India during British Period in a Historical Perspective, International Journal of Management, 11(9), 2020, pp. 1464-1470.http://iaeme.com/Home/issue/IJM?Volume=11&Issue=9

Meena, R. P. (2022). *Indian History: Latest Current Affairs Yearbook 2020.* IAS INSIGHTS.

Mishra, A. (2011, February 6). *INDIA: Charity not beginning at home for universities.* University World News. https://www.universityworldnews.com/post.php?story=20110204222722977

Mushtaq M. U. (2009). Public health in british India: a brief account of the history of medical services and disease prevention in colonial India. *Indian journal of community medicine : official publication of Indian Association of Preventive & Social Medicine, 34*(1), 6–14. https://doi.org/10.4103/0970-0218.45369

N Pandya, D. R. (2014). Indian Education System- A Historical Journey. *International Journal for Research in Education, 3*(3).

Nurulla, S., & Naik, J.P. (1971). *A history of education in India during the British period.* Macmillan.

Poddar, G. (2020, June 16). *Philanthropy-based universities | New temples of learning?* Deccan Herald. https://www.deccanherald.com/opinion/main-article/philanthropy-based-universities-new-temples-of-learning-850411.html

Ravi Kumar, V. (n.d.). *Destruction of the Indian System of Education.* http://home.iitk.ac.in/~hcverma/Article/Article%20by%20IITM%20student%20in%20Indian%20education.pdf

Roy, H., & Alam, J. (2021). *A History of Colonial India: 1757 to 1947.* Taylor & Francis.

Roy, T. (2015). British Rule and the Indian Village. *Economic and Political Weekly, 29*(7), 7–8. https://www.epw.in/journal/1994/7/reviews-uncategorised/british-rule-and-indian-village.html

Sahni, J. (2020). *Magbook Indian History 2020.* Arihant Publications India limited.

Sharma, K. (2021, August 21). *Indian universities are being taught how to generate funds like Harvard & Cambridge.* ThePrint. https://theprint.in/india/education/indian-universities-are-being-taught-how-to-generate-funds-like-harvard-cambridge/719113/

Simha, R. K. (2016, April 30). *Forget Kohinoor, The British Looted Greater Treasures From India.* Swarajyamag. https://swarajyamag.com/world/forget-kohinoor-the-british-looted-greater-treasures-from-india

SPODEK, H. (2013). City Planning in India under British Rule. *Economic and Political Weekly, 48*(4), 53–61. http://www.jstor.org/stable/23391350

Sundar, P. (2022, February 21). *Reforming Higher Education, With a Helping Hand From Philanthropy.* The Wire. https://thewire.in/education/reforming-higher-education-with-a-helping-hand-from-philanthropy

Weber, T. (1997). *On the Salt March: The Historiography of Gandhi's March to Dandi.* HarperCollins Publishers India.

Wolpert, S. A. (2020, September 8). British raj. Encyclopedia Britannica. https://www.britannica.com/event/British-raj

Chapter 3: Education – A Privilege for Independent India

Ahmad Ganie, R., & Mohi Ud Din, T. (2015). Impact of Insurgency on Education in Kashmir. In *Internet Archive.* Journal of Education and Practice. https://archive.org/details/ERIC_EJ1083854

Altbach, P. G. (1966). The Transformation of the Indian Student Movement. *Asian Survey, 6*(8), 448–460. https://doi.org/10.2307/2642471

Banerjee, R. (2016, July 3). *A class war gone wrong.* Theweek.in. https://www.theweek.in/theweek/cover/naxalbari-movement.html

Beno, Michal. (2019). The implications of the Industrial Revolutions for Higher Education.

Britannica, T. Editors of Encyclopaedia (2018, June 20). Portuguese India. Encyclopedia Britannica. https://www.britannica.com/place/Portuguese-India

Deivam, D. M. (2020, September 11). *Education in the post independence period.* https://www.slideshare.net/deivammuniyandi/education-in-the-post-independence-period

Disha. (2014, December 22). *Higher Education in Independent India.* Your Article Library. https://www.yourarticlelibrary.com/education/higher-education-in-independent-india/44852

Dutta, Hitakshi & Kanwar, Varinder. (2020). Redefining Indian Universities: An Insight of Education Sector towards Evolution of Industry 4.0 and 5.0. 58. 45-49.

Hilton, Adriel Adon; McClain, Kevin; and Outten, Donavan L. (2018) "The Industrial Revolution of Higher Education," *Journal of Research Initiatives*: Vol. 3, Iss. 3, Article 12.Available at: https://digitalcommons.uncfsu.edu/jri/vol3/iss3/12

IANS. (2014, August 22). Don't copy us, Mao had told Indian Maoists. *Business Standard India.* https://www.business-standard.com/article/news-ians/don-t-copy-us-mao-had-told-indian-maoists-114082200217_1.html

Anti-Hindi agitations of Tamil Nadu. (2022, August 4). Wikipedia. https://en.wikipedia.org/wiki/Anti-Hindi_agitations_of_Tamil_Nadu

Azad Hind. (2022, October 1). Wikipedia. https://en.wikipedia.org/wiki/Azad_Hind

Education – The postindependence period in India. (n.d.). Encyclopedia Britannica. https://www.britannica.com/topic/education/The-postindependence-period-in-India

Hari Singh. (2020, January 10). Wikipedia; Wikimedia Foundation. https://en.wikipedia.org/wiki/Hari_Singh

Home Page : IIT Delhi. (n.d.). Home.iitd.ac.in. Retrieved October 4, 2022, from https://home.iitd.ac.in/index.php

IIT Kanpur. (2022, July 17). Wikipedia. https://en.wikipedia.org/wiki/IIT_Kanpur

Indian Institute of Science. (2019, November 15). Wikipedia; Wikimedia Foundation. https://en.wikipedia.org/wiki/Indian_Institute_of_Science

Indian Institute of Science. (2022). https://iisc.ac.in/

Indian Institute of Technology Bombay | IIT Bombay. (n.d.). Www.iitb.ac.in. Retrieved October 4, 2022, from https://www.iitb.ac.in/

Indian Institute of Technology Kharagpur. (n.d.). Www.iitkgp.ac.in. Retrieved October 4, 2022, from http://www.iitkgp.ac.in/

Indian Institute of Technology Madras, Tamilnadu. (2019). Iitm.ac.in. https://www.iitm.ac.in/

Indian National Army. (2021, February 9). Wikipedia. https://en.wikipedia.org/wiki/Indian_National_Army

Jammu and Kashmir (union territory). (2022, September 30). Wikipedia. https://en.wikipedia.org/wiki/Jammu_and_Kashmir_(union_territory)#:~:text=A%20resolution%20to%20repeal%20Article

Kashmiri Pandits. (2022, August 16). Wikipedia. https://en.wikipedia.org/wiki/Kashmiri_Pandits

List of Indian engineering colleges before Independence. (2022, September 11). Wikipedia. https://en.wikipedia.org/wiki/List_of_Indian_engineering_colleges_before_Independence

Mahatma Gandhi said, "If someone slaps you on one side of your face, turn the other one to him." Would you show your other side, slap bac... (n.d.). Quora. Retrieved October 3, 2022, from https://www.quora.com/Mahatma-Gandhi-said-%E2%80%9CIf-someone-slaps-you-on-one-side-of-your-face-turn-the-other-one-to-him-Would-you-show-your-other-side-slap-back-or-do-something-different

Naxalite–Maoist insurgency. (2022, September 22). Wikipedia; Wikimedia Foundation. https://en.wikipedia.org/wiki/Naxalite%E2%80%93Maoist_insurgency#:~:text=The%20term%20Naxal%20comes%20from

ONE HUNDRED TAMILS OF THE 20TH CENTURY. (1979). Annamalai University Golden Jubilee Souvenir.

Sabotaged Schooling : Naxalite Attacks and Police Occupation of Schools in India's Bihar and Jharkhand States. (2009). Human Rights Watch.

Seven oldest universities in India: All you need to know. (2015, September 22). India Today. https://www.indiatoday.in/education-today/featurephilia/story/oldest-universities-264121-2015-09-21

Jan 18, P. (2016, January 18). *President ask youths to adopt Netaji's message of faith, unity and sacrifice | India News - Times of India*. The Times of India. https://timesofindia.indiatimes.com/india/president-ask-youths-to-adopt-netajis-message-of-faith-unity-and-sacrifice/articleshow/50628418.cms

Khan, Y. (2017). *The Great Partition : the making of India and Pakistan*. Yale University Press.

Kumar, D.M., & Rekha, D.N. (2020). *Historical And Political Economy Of Education In India*. Sankalp Publication.

Mahajan, V. D. (1946). Why Has Local Self-Government Failed in India? *The Indian Journal of Political Science*, *7*(4), 521–527. http://www.jstor.org/stable/42743138

Mahmood, S. (1895). *A History of English Education in India: Its Rise, Development, Progress, Present Condition and Prospects, Being a Narrative of the Various Phases of Educational Policy and Measures Adopted Under the British Rule from Its Beginning to the Present Period, (1781 to 1893)*. M.A.O. College.

Mushtaq M. U. (2009). Public health in british India: a brief account of the history of medical services and disease prevention in colonial India. *Indian journal of community medicine : official publication of Indian Association of Preventive & Social Medicine*, *34*(1), 6–14. https://doi.org/10.4103/0970-0218.45369

Press Information Bureau of India. (2016, January 16). *President of India urges youth to adopt slogan of itmad, ittefaq andkurbani which Netaji gave to the soldiers and civilian personnel of the Azad Hind Fauj*. Pib.gov.in. https://pib.gov.in/newsite/PrintRelease.aspx?relid=134576

Roffelsen, C. (2016, September 25). *How Nehru Shaped India's Development*. Medium. https://medium.com/@ceesroffelsen/how-nehru-shaped-indias-development-4df38535bf98

Sircar, J. (2021, March 11). *In a Calcutta Gripped With Naxal Violence and Police Brutality, People Lost Sons, Brothers and Friends*. The Wire. https://thewire.in/history/calcutta-naxal-violence-police-brutality-1971

Talbot, I., & Singh, G. (2014). *The partition of India*. Cambridge University Press.

Thakore, D. (2021, August 11). *"I believe Nehru's greatest failure was to ignore primary education..."* EducationWorld. https://www.educationworld.in/i-believe-nehrus-greatest-failure-was-to-ignore-primary-education/

Washbrook, D.A. (1982). Ethnicity and Racialism in Colonial Indian Society. In: Ross, R. (eds) Racism and Colonialism. Comparative Studies in Overseas History, vol 4. Springer, Dordrecht. https://doi.org/10.1007/978-94-009-7544-6_9

Yeravdekar, Vidya and Tiwari, Gauri, The Higher Education System in India and Its Impact on the Economy (September 1, 2012). Available at SSRN: https://ssrn.com/abstract=2139894 or http://dx.doi.org/10.2139/ssrn.2139894

Chapter 4: Reforms of Independent India – A Resource-constrained Long Battle Towards Literacy

Development of School Education Status in India - Scientific Figure on ResearchGate. Available from: https://www.researchgate.net/figure/Enrolment-in-schools-in-the-year-1993-and-2002_tbl3_321220159

Arjun Singh (Madhya Pradesh politician). (2022, September 21). Wikipedia. https://en.wikipedia.org/wiki/Arjun_Singh_(Madhya_Pradesh_politician)

Atal Bihari Vajpayee. (2019, December 2). Wikipedia; Wikimedia Foundation. https://en.wikipedia.org/wiki/Atal_Bihari_Vajpayee

Central university (India). (2022, September 13). Wikipedia. https://en.wikipedia.org/wiki/Central_university_(India)

Constitution of India. (2019, April 6). Wikipedia; Wikimedia Foundation. https://en.wikipedia.org/wiki/Constitution_of_India

Dharmendra Pradhan. (2022, September 21). Wikipedia. https://en.wikipedia.org/wiki/Dharmendra_Pradhan

Education in India 1993-1994 Report. (1993). Ministry of Human Resource Development. http://14.139.60.153/handle/123456789/2573?mode=full

Education Ministers Of India | List of Education Minister of India From 1947 to 2019. (n.d.). Reviewadda. Retrieved October 4, 2022, from https://www.reviewadda.com/institute/article/64/education-ministers-of-india

Education ministers of India since independence. (2021, July 9). EducationWorld. https://www.educationworld.in/education-ministers-of-india-since-independence/

Government of India, Ministry of Education. (n.d.). Www.education.gov.in. https://www.education.gov.in/

Humayun Kabir. (2022, September 20). Wikipedia. https://en.wikipedia.org/wiki/Humayun_Kabir

Indian National Congress. (n.d.). Indian National Congress. Retrieved October 4, 2022, from https://inc.in/congress-sandesh/achievement/world-class-educational-institutes-in-india-is-the-gift-of-congress-government

Kapil Sibal. (2022, October 2). Wikipedia. https://en.wikipedia.org/wiki/Kapil_Sibal

K.C. Pant. (2022, September 21). Wikipedia. https://en.wikipedia.org/wiki/K._C._Pant

K.L. Shrimali. (2022, September 20). Wikipedia. https://en.wikipedia.org/wiki/K._L._Shrimali

Madhavrao Scindia. (2019, June 9). Wikipedia; Wikimedia Foundation. https://en.wikipedia.org/wiki/Madhavrao_Scindia

M.C. Chagla. (2022, September 25). Wikipedia. https://en.wikipedia.org/wiki/M._C._Chagla

Ministry of Education (India). (2022, September 29). Wikipedia. https://en.wikipedia.org/wiki/Ministry_of_Education_(India)

M.M. Pallam Raju. (2022, September 21). Wikipedia. https://en.wikipedia.org/wiki/M._M._Pallam_Raju

Murli Manohar Joshi. (2022, September 21). Wikipedia. https://en.wikipedia.org/wiki/Murli_Manohar_Joshi

National Education Policy 2020. (2020). Ministry of Education. https://www.education.gov.in/sites/upload_files/mhrd/files/NEP_Final_English_0.pdf

Prakash Javadekar. (2022, September 17). Wikipedia. https://en.wikipedia.org/wiki/Prakash_Javadekar

Pratap Chandra Chunder. (2022, September 20). Wikipedia. https://en.wikipedia.org/wiki/Pratap_Chandra_Chunder

P. Shiv Shankar. (2022, September 21). Wikipedia. https://en.wikipedia.org/wiki/P._Shiv_Shankar

P.V. Narasimha Rao. (2021, June 11). Wikipedia. https://en.wikipedia.org/wiki/P._V._Narasimha_Rao

Raj Mangal Pande. (2022, September 21). Wikipedia. https://en.wikipedia.org/wiki/Raj_Mangal_Pande

Ramesh Pokhriyal. (2022, September 21). Wikipedia. https://en.wikipedia.org/wiki/Ramesh_Pokhriyal

Saiyid Nurul Hasan. (2022, September 18). Wikipedia. https://en.wikipedia.org/wiki/Saiyid_Nurul_Hasan

Shankarrao Chavan. (2019, November 8). Wikipedia; Wikimedia Foundation. https://en.wikipedia.org/wiki/Shankarrao_Chavan

Sheila Kaul. (2022, September 21). Wikipedia. https://en.wikipedia.org/wiki/Sheila_Kaul

Siddhartha Shankar Ray. (2022, September 27). Wikipedia. https://en.wikipedia.org/wiki/Siddhartha_Shankar_Ray

Smriti Irani. (2019, December 25). Wikipedia; Wikimedia Foundation. https://en.wikipedia.org/wiki/Smriti_Irani

S. R. Bommai. (2022, September 17). Wikipedia. https://en.wikipedia.org/wiki/S._R._Bommai

State university (India). (2022, July 20). Wikipedia. https://en.wikipedia.org/wiki/State_university_(India)

Triguna Sen. (2022, April 21). Wikipedia. https://en.wikipedia.org/wiki/Triguna_Sen

UGC, New Delhi, India. (2020). Ugc.ac.in. https://www.ugc.ac.in/

University of Calcutta. (n.d.). Www.caluniv.ac.in. Retrieved October 4, 2022, from https://www.caluniv.ac.in/

Vishwanath Pratap Singh. (2019, August 17). Wikipedia; Wikimedia Foundation. https://en.wikipedia.org/wiki/V._P._Singh

VJTI Mumbai – Veermata Jijabai Technological Institute. (n.d.). Vjti.ac.in. Retrieved October 4, 2022, from https://vjti.ac.in/

V.K.R.V. Rao. (2022, September 20). Wikipedia. https://en.wikipedia.org/wiki/V._K._R._V._Rao

M. K. Singh. (2009). *Encyclopaedia of Indian War of Independence, 1857-1947: The architects of Indian Constitution : Dr. Bhim Rao Ambedkar, Dr. Rajendra Prasad and Maulana Abul Kalam Azad.* Anmol Publications.

Padalkar, R. (2021). *Ruling Dynasties of Independent India – Volume 1.* Notion Press.

Paul, S. (2022, February 25). *What did Nehru's public sectors do for India?* Times of India Blog. https://timesofindia.indiatimes.com/blogs/courts-commerce-and-the-constitution/what-did-nehrus-public-sectors-do-for-india/

Press Information Bureau PIB. (2022, February 1). *Shri Dharmendra Pradhan lauds Budget 2022 as inclusive, forward looking and aspirational.* Pib.gov.in. https://pib.gov.in/Pressreleaseshare.aspx?PRID=1794484

Shankar, G. (2022). *Women who Ruled the World- ancient to contemporary times.* Gyan Shankar.

Singh, H. (2017). *Leading the Change--: 50 Years of NCERT.* National Council of Educational Research and Training, 2011.

What is India's caste system? (2019, June 19). *BBC News.* https://www.bbc.com/news/world-asia-india-35650616

Chapter 5: The Resurgence – India, a Step Closer to Being a Knowledge Superpower

Al-Youbi, A., H. M. Zahed, A., & G. Tierney, W. (2020). *Successful Global Collaborations in Higher Education Institutions.* Springer International Publishing. https://doi.org/10.1007/978-3-030-25525-1

Diwakar Education Hub. (2022). *UGC NET economics unit-8.* Divakar Education Hub.

Annual Report 2016-2017. (2017). Ministry of Human Resource Development.

Demand for Grants 2022-23 Analysis : Education. (n.d.). PRS Legislative Research. https://prsindia.org/budgets/parliament/demand-for-grants-2022-23-analysis-education

Enabling Glocalisation of Indian Higher Education, New Delhi, March 29, 2017 | Unescochair. (2017, April 25). https://www.unescochair-cbrsr.org/enabling-glocalisation-of-indian-higher-education-new-delhi-march-29-2017/

Government approves Rashtriya Uchchatar Shiksha Abhiyan (RUSA) Scheme to continue till 31st March, 2026. (2022, February 18). Pib.gov.in. https://pib.gov.in/PressReleaseIframePage.aspx?PRID=1799301

Government of India, All India Council for Technical Education |. (n.d.). Www.aicte-India.org. https://www.aicte-india.org

Government of India, Ministry of Education. (n.d.). Www.education.gov.in. https://www.education.gov.in

Guidelines for Internationalisation of Higher Education. (2021). University Grants Commission. https://www.education.gov.in/sites/upload_files/mhrd/files/upload_document/int_he.pdf

Household Social Consumption on Education in India Government of India. (2017). Ministry of Statistics and Programme Implementation. http://mospi.nic.in/sites/default/files/publication_reports/Report_585_75th_round_Education_final_1507_0.pdf

Ministry of Education (India). (2022, September 29). Wikipedia. https://en.wikipedia.org/wiki/Ministry_of_Education_(India)#:~:text=Under%20the%20NEP%20 2020%2C%20the

Nalanda University. (2022, September 2). Wikipedia. https://en.wikipedia.org/wiki/Nalanda_University

National Scholarship Portal. (n.d.). Scholarships.gov.in. Retrieved October 4, 2022, from https://scholarships.gov.in/

NPTEL, online courses and certification, Learn for free. (2019). Nptel.ac.in. https://nptel.ac.in/

Rashtriya Uchchatar Shiksha Abhiyan (RUSA). (n.d.). Www.manoramayearbook.in. Retrieved October 4, 2022, from https://www.manoramayearbook.in/current-affairs/india/2022/02/19/rashtriya-uchchatar-shiksha-abhiyan-rusa.html#:~:text=Rashtriya%20Uchchatar%20Shiksha%20Abhiyan%20(RUSA)%20was%20approved%20in%20October%202013.&text=It%20is%20an%20overarching%20scheme

Sub-Mission on Polytechnics under the Coordinated Action for Skill Development The Ministry of Human Resource Development has launched a Nation wide Scheme on "Sub-Mission on Polytechnics" under Co-ordinated Action for Skill Development in order to augment Skilled Manpower requirement in the. (n.d.). Retrieved October 4, 2022, from http://pibmumbai.gov.in/english/pdf/e0000_h124.pdf

Swayam Central. (n.d.). Swayam.gov.in. https://swayam.gov.in/

MasterSoft. (n.d.). *What is Academic Bank of Credits (ABC) in Higher Education Institutions?* Www.iitms.co.in. Retrieved October 4, 2022, from https://www.iitms.co.in/blog/what-is-academic-bank-of-credit.html

Nangia, V. (2020, November 16). *Institutes of National Importance (INI), Institutions of Eminence (IoE) and National Education Policy (NEP) 2020.* Vinay Nangia. https://vinaynangia.com/2020/11/16/institutes-of-national-importance-ini-institutions-of-eminence-ioe-and-national-education-policy-nep-2020/

Nikam, D. M., & Pawar, D. A. (2021). Discourse on Higher Education Research & Teaching Learning. In *Google Books.* Sankalp Publication.

Patel, F., & Lynch, H. (n.d.). *Glocalization as an Alternative to Internationalization in Higher Education: Embedding Positive Glocal Learning Perspectives* (2013th ed.). International Journal of Teaching and Learning in Higher Education.

PIB. (2022, February 2). *Status of National Initiative for Design Innovation.* Pib.gov.in. https://pib.gov.in/PressReleasePage.aspx?PRID=1794747

PTI. (2012, December 6). *Govt approves 20 new IITs in Public-Private Partnership model.* India Today. https://www.indiatoday.in/parliament/story/govt-approves-20-new-iits-in-public-private-partnership-model-123496-2012-12-06

PTI. (2020, August 18). HRD Ministry is now officially Education Ministry as President approves name change. *The Hindu*. https://www.thehindu.com/news/national/president-gives-nod-to-hrd-ministry-name-change/article32380281.ece

Shahani, D. A. (2022, March 24). *How can India achieve universal literacy as per the UN's Sustainable Development Goal 4?* Financialexpress. https://www.financialexpress.com/education-2/how-can-india-achieve-universal-literacy-as-per-the-uns-sustainable-development-goal-4/2470535/

Yadav, S. (2020, July 31). *Explained: How India's Education Ministry became "HRD Ministry", and then returned to embrace Education*. The Indian Express. https://indianexpress.com/article/explained/explained-hrd-ministry-and-ministry-of-education-6531694/

Yeravdekar, Vidya and Tiwari, Gauri, The Higher Education System in India and Its Impact on the Economy (September 1, 2012). Available at SSRN: https://ssrn.com/abstract=2139894 or http://dx.doi.org/10.2139/ssrn.2139894

Afterword

Since 2014, the university rankings of Indian universities have been on the rise according to QS World University Rankings. In fact, India now has 27 universities in the top 1,000 in the 2023 edition announced in June 2022. This is great news for students looking to study in India, as they now have more options when it comes to choosing a university. There are a number of reasons why Indian universities have seen such a dramatic increase in rankings. One of the main reasons is that more and more Indian universities are starting to invest in research and development. This is resulting in better-quality research being produced by Indian universities, which is then being recognised by academia and recruiters globally, which have a direct impact in the QS World University Rankings. Another reason for the increase in university rankings is the increasing number of international students who are choosing to study in India. This is because India offers a great mix of world-class education at a fraction of the cost of studying in other developed countries.

In the top-200 universities by QS World University Rankings released in 2022, Indian Institute of Science (IISc) ranked first in the list for research. Joining it, two other Indian Institutions—Indian Institute of Technology (IIT), Bombay, and Indian Institute of Technology (IIT), Delhi—were in the top-200 overall. Even after securing top spots in the research indicator, many Indian universities lack in academic reputation. India is great at bringing top research but the low academic reputation is concerning. The world cannot ignore the great potential of the current Indian education system and the Indian universities hold.

Furthermore, QS World University Rankings by Subject provides a comparison of the performance of 15,200 specific university programmes taken by students from 1,543 universities in 88 locations throughout the world, across 51 academic fields and 5 main faculty areas.

Several Indian universities and institutions have been included in the QS World University Rankings by Subject Rankings for 2022. Academic reputation, employer reputation, research citations per publication, h-index, and international research network are among the 5 factors used to rank universities in this separate rankings by subject.

QS Research Director Ben Sowter has said: 'Several programmes at India's privately run Institutes of Eminence have made progress this year, demonstrating the positive role that well-regulated private provision can have in enhancing India's higher education sector.'

The Academic Ranking of World Universities (ARWU) is a widely recognised ranking system for higher education institutions. In the most recent ARWU rankings, not a single Indian university was included in the top 100. This lack of representation is surprising, given that India is home to some of the world's top research institutions. In fact, India is the second-largest producer of scientific research papers, after the United States. The ARWU rankings place a lot of importance on the number of Nobel laureates and fields medalists associated with a university. And while Indian universities have produced some world-renowned researchers, they haven't been as successful in attracting Nobel laureates and fields medalists.

Indian universities need to focus on academic rankings if India wants to be a knowledge superpower. India has some of the world's top universities, but they are not ranked highly in international rankings. This is a problem because academic rankings are one of the main ways that nations are judged on their commitment to knowledge and research.

Some of the focus areas include investing more in research, improving infrastructure, and attracting more world-class faculty. It is also important to create an environment that is conducive to learning and research. Indian universities have made great strides in recent years, but there is still a long way to go.

Even though have not achieved a top-100 status, they will continue to be important players in the global higher education landscape.

Global rankings have become the de facto standard for evaluating an institution's quality and academic rigour. It is a big thing for Indian universities to rank among the world's top 200 universities and the need of pursuing changes that will pave the way for advancing excellence in higher education and research. It is critical for Indian universities to adopt the global rankings systems as well as international accreditation processes, which will allow Indian universities to be benchmarked against world-class universities. The best is yet to come!

About the Author

Dr Ashwin Fernandes is an ambassador of the quality movement in education and has advocated the need for independent evaluation mechanisms for promoting excellence. He actively advocates the use of rankings, accreditation and other QA models for various purposes, be it for students aspiring for higher education in reputed institutions across the globe or government agencies looking to have their universities compete globally or academics looking for partners focused on research initiatives.

Ashwin is regional director for Africa, Middle East, and South Asia at QS Quacquarelli Symonds – the world's largest international education network. He works closely with institutions across the regions to better understand the local context and to support the drive for excellence and capacity building.

During his professional engagement, he has met with senior leaders from the region and is often invited to speak at several conferences and events on university rankings, ratings, education, higher education etc. He has been a panellist on various discussion forums and presented his recommendations on thought provoking topics related to higher education.

Dr Fernandes founded India's first nationwide private sector evaluation framework called QS I-GAUGE. He has a Doctorate of Philosophy (D.Phil) along with a MBA in Marketing and a B.Com degree in Financial Accounting, Auditing & Taxation. He has lived and worked in 5 countries and visited over 300 educational institutions in his 11 years at QS.